EXPERT EVIDENCE UNDER THE CPR:

A Compendium of Cases from April 1999 to
April 2001

£2-50
GC

10/8.

AUSTRALIA
LBC Information Services Ltd
Sydney

CANADA AND USA
Carswell
Toronto

NEW ZEALAND
Brooker's
· Auckland

SINGAPORE and MALAYSIA
Sweet & Maxwell Asia
Singapore and Kuala Lumpur

EXPERT EVIDENCE UNDER THE CPR:

A Compendium of Cases from April 1999 to
April 2001

Joanna Day
Solicitor

Louise Le Gat
Solicitor

ALLEN & OVERY

EWI

LONDON
SWEET & MAXWELL
2001

Published in 2001 by
Sweet & Maxwell Limited of
100 Avenue Road,
Swiss Cottage,
NW3 3PF
Typeset by J&L Composition, Filey, North Yorkshire
and Printed and bound in Great Britain by MPG Books Ltd, Bodmin, Cornwall

No natural forests were destroyed to make this product;
only farmed timber was used and replanted

A CIP *catalogue record for this book*
is available from the British Library

ISBN 0421 768 304

The content of this book is for general guidance only and does not contain
definitive legal advice.

Whilst every care has been taken to establish and acknowledge copyright,
and contact the copyright owners, the publishers tender their apologies for any
accidental infringement. They would be pleased to come to suitable
arrangement with the owners in each case.

Table of Contents

Foreword

The opinion of a properly qualified expert on an issue within his or her field of expertise can often give a judge invaluable help in finding a sound answer to problems arising in the course of litigation. But like all procedural tools expert opinion evidence, invaluable if properly used, can be improperly used; and then it can disfigure the litigious process by causing delay, unnecessary expense and contamination of what should be independent and objective expert opinion by considerations of partisan advantage.

An important aim of the Civil Procedure Rules is to curb the abuses to which misuse of expert evidence has given rise in the past while ensuring that the courts continue to enjoy the help which such evidence alone can give. This interesting and informative compendium of the recent case law is an interim report on progress so far. Reading the summary, one is stuck by two points in particular. First, there has been an extra ordinary glut of decisions, clearly demonstrating the importance which litigating parties attach to issues concerning expert evidence. Money would not be spent disputing these issues if parties did not think they really mattered. But secondly, the decisions of the courts show that the new rules are making a demonstrable impact on practices and habits of thought which were once tolerated but no longer are. Many of these cases would, until quite recently, have been decided differently. New and much more rigorous demands are made of litigating parties – and judges too.

Some of the decisions summarised here are reported, others not. Whether reported or not, the decisions highlight the benefits of good professional practice and the penalties paid by those who fail to think ahead, fail to observe the rules and casually assume that the bad old habits of the past will continue to pass muster.

Here then, is a chart which clearly marks the navigable channel and marks also the sites of previous wrecks and marine casualties. The wise pilot will study the chart – to the immense benefit of passengers, cargo, crew and harbour-master.

Lord Bingham

Preface

"The subject of expert witnesses has figured prominently throughout the consultative process. Apart from discovery it was the subject which caused most concern . . . The need to engage experts was a source of excessive expense, delay and, in some cases, increased complexity through excessive or inappropriate use of experts" (Interim Report on Access to Justice (June 1995), Chapter 23, para. 1).

Expert evidence was one of the most challenging areas considered during the reassessment of civil procedure. Wide-ranging reforms were introduced in this area. The key was a re-emphasis on the true duty of the expert to inform the court rather than to justify the position of the party paying his fees. When the then new Civil Procedure Rules ("CPR") came into force, there was concern at the concept of the single joint expert, the strong desire to keep expert evidence to a minimum and the requirement to inform the court of expert availability on allocation of the case. This compendium of cases examines the cases addressing these and other issues.

The CPR have now been operating for just over two years and, unsurprisingly, expert evidence has generated a high level of case law at appellate level. Lord Woolf himself sat on the bench of nearly 10 per cent of the cases in this compendium. The case law included in this compendium shows that the role and duties of experts is indeed evolving, mainly as a result of the court's emphasis on proportionality. The courts are now taking a firmer hand regarding all aspects of expert evidence: whether it should be allowed at all; its usefulness; its timing; and of course its cost. Expert evidence will only be allowed if it is really needed (*i.e.* there is a need for specialist knowledge), and if it is, it should not be used more than is necessary. Some practical advice from May L.J.: "Go to the heart of the matter. Leave out inessentials. If you have to write a report, keep it succinct".

The reduced *use* of expert evidence is, however, not to be perceived as diminishing the value of expert evidence. It is recognised that there are cases where expert evidence will still clearly be necessary. Judges cannot be experts in everything. In those cases, the Court of Appeal has been careful to warn judges to pay sufficient attention to the expert evidence before them and to give reasons for preferring one expert's evidence to another's.

The impact of the CPR on expert evidence can also be assessed by reviewing the extent to which some individual rules have been effectively applied in the course of the last two years:

- **Expert's duty to the court:** the Access to Justice Final Report recommended a new approach which emphasised the expert's impartiality and this is embodied in CPR r.35.3. As May L.J. highlighted in his keynote address to the EWI annual conference in October 2001: "you [experts] have an overriding duty to the court . . . a duty which overrides any obligation to the person from whom you have received instructions or by whom you are paid. You are not there to engage in a sparring match with your opposite number." The courts have actively upheld this duty by criticising expert witnesses where they have shown signs of partiality.

There were initially concerns that this duty would entail the appointment of "shadow" experts with whom a party could discuss the full merits of his case without concern that those discussions could be stripped of privilege. This does not seem to have materialised before the courts although anecdotal evidence suggests it is happening to a certain extent behind the scenes.

- **The single joint expert:** CPR r.35.7 introduced the concept of the single joint expert. The idea was that parties were strongly encouraged to try to agree on an expert to instruct. Where this was not possible, the court could select a single joint expert to act in the case. This struck horror in the hearts of many. One of the strong concerns in this area was that costs would spiral as a result of the need in complex cases to appoint experts for each party as well as the single joint experts, the costs of which would be irrecoverable.

In fact, the concept of the single joint expert has been creatively adapted to suit different matters and courts. The courts have in this context recognised that, whilst taking into account the possibility of appointing a single joint expert, there are many multi-track cases which, by virtue of their complexity and the sums at stake, will still warrant each party having its own expert.

- **Written questions to experts**: the courts have enthusiastically taken up the spirit of written questions to experts provided for by CPR r.35.6, whereby a party may put to the other side's expert or a single joint expert written questions about his report. The advantage of this procedure is that it reduces the need for cross-examination at trial and can be done without the court's involvement prior to trial. We expect that this is an area of the new procedure which is as yet still under-used.

All in all, the courts seem to have embraced the changes encompassed in the CPR relating to expert evidence. Looking to the future, we expect that there will be further developments in the areas of immunity for experts and conflicts of interest for experts. In addition, further innovations are expected:

- the introduction of a new Code of Guidance on Expert Evidence which is intended to facilitate better communication and dealings both between the expert and the instructing party and between the parties; and

- further changes to the CPR to match more closely the practice for experts in the Commercial Court relating to, for example, duties of experts and the content and form of their reports.

This area therefore promises to remain an area of activity and scrutiny in the years to come until the courts can feel confident that the ills identified in the reports leading up to the CPR have been fully remedied.

Although this compendium could not include every case which has raised issues of expert evidence since the introduction of the CPR, it draws a comprehensive selection of the cases, organised into 12 sections, covering different subjects such as single joint experts and admissibility. Within each section the cases are ordered chronologically. The case reports cover the ground between a headnote and the judgment itself. They contain quotes from the judges so that you can see what they are saying, in their own words. At the beginning of each section, we have tied together the threads of the individual cases to create a short introduction. This is not a textbook dealing with all areas relevant to expert witnesses — we have let the cases guide the selection of subjects covered.

Joanna Day and Louise Le Gat

About the Authors

Joanna Day joined Allen & Overy in 1996. She qualified into the corporate and commercial litigation group in March 1998. Joanna's experience covers general commercial litigation and mediation for major corporate and banking clients. She now works as a professional support lawyer.

Louise Le Gat has been an associate in the litigation and dispute resolution department since 1998. She is part of the corporate and commercial group. She is bilingual in French and English and has therefore dealt with a range of disputes involving French entities and/or French clients.

About Allen & Overy

Allen & Overy is a premier international law firm. Founded in 1930, we now have over 4000 staff, including some 390 partners working in 25 major centres worldwide. We meet the requirements of businesses, financiers and governments whenever there is a need for decisive legal advice on complex matters from experienced international lawyers.

Our global litigation and dispute resolution practice, with almost 90 partners worldwide, gives advice and practical guidance to clients involved in actual or potential disputes. Our aim is to help clients resolve disputes before they escalate, but we like to advise how to prevent disputes arising in the first place. In the event that a dispute is unavoidable, we work with our clients to seek the best means of resolving it: where litigation or arbitration becomes necessary, we pursue the case with diligence and vigour; where appropriate, we promote the use of alternative dispute resolution methods.

Our litigation department aims not simply to advise on what cannot be done, but to think imaginatively and constructively in order to ensure that our clients' commercial objectives are met and that their interests and reputations are protected. We seek to establish and maintain a high level of personal contact with our clients, to anticipate developments and to stretch ourselves in order to perform above our clients' expectations.

Visit Allen & Overy at: *www.allenovery.com*

About the Expert Witness Institute

"The Expert Witness Institute has made remarkable strides within a short space of time, confirming the view that expert witnesses have a need for the services which it is offering": Lord Woolf, Lord Chief Justice.

The Expert Witness Institute ("EWI") was launched in November 1996 in response to the demands of experts. The objective of the EWI is the support of the proper administration of justice and the early resolution of disputes through fair and unbiased expert evidence.

To achieve this objective, the EWI:

- acts as a voice for expert witnesses, especially in communicating with the media;

- provides support to experts of all professional disciplines and other occupations requiring skills and judgement;

- encourages lawyers to make use of experts wherever specialist knowledge is required;

- engages in the training of experts to maintain and enhance standards and their status;

- works actively with other allied professional bodies and associations; and

- make representations to Government and to professional bodies and associations wherever appropriate.

EWI differs from other experts' organisations in that it has a Professional Bodies Advisory Group. The EWI works with professional bodies to support their expert groups, set standards and represent their views, and in turn the professional bodies assist the EWI with advice and suggestions.

Through the EWI, members have access to education and training courses. 'Basic Law for Expert Witnesses' has been designed in conjunction with the University of Liverpool Law Faculty. The EWI has also approved intensive courses in courtroom skills and report writing.

The EWI is a non-profit-making company limited by guarantee. No commercial organisation has any representative on the Governing Body. Its independence and integrity are guaranteed by the Board of Directors (Governors).

The Expert Witness Institute
Africa House
64–78 Kingsway
London
WC2B 6BD

Tel: 020 7405 5854
Fax: 020 7405 5850
Email: *info@ewi.org.uk*
Web site at *www.EWI.org.uk*

Table of Abbreviations

A.C.	Appeal Cases
All E.R.	All England Law Reports
All E.R. (Comm)	All England Law Reports (Commercial Cases)
B.C.L.C.	Butterworths Company Law Cases
B.L.R.	Building Law Reports
Ch.	Chancery Law Reports
C.I.L.L.	Construction Industry Law Letter
Con. L.R.	Construction Law Reports
C.P.L.R.	Civil Practice Law Reports
C.P. Rep.	Civil Procedure Reports (online)
Crim. L.R.	Criminal Law Review
E.G.	Estates Gazette
E.G.C.S.	Estates Gazette Case Summaries
E.G.L.R.	Estates Gazette Law Reports
Env. L.R.	Environmental Law Reports
E.W.C.A. Civ.	England and Wales Court of Appeal (Civil Division)
E.W.H.C. Admin.	England and Wales High Court (Administrative Court)
F.L.R.	Family Law Reports
F.S.R.	Fleet Street Reports
The Independent	The Independent Law Reports
I.P.D.	Intellectual Property Decisions
I.R.L.R.	Industrial Relations Law Reports
Lloyd's Rep.	Lloyd's Law Reports
Lloyd's Rep. Bank	Lloyd's Law Reports Banking
Lloyd's Rep. Med	Lloyd's Law Reports Medical
Lloyd's Rep. P.N.	Lloyd's Law Reports Professional Negligence
Med. L.R.	Medical Law Reports
N.Z.L.R.	New Zealand Law Reports
P.I.Q.R.	Personal Injuries and Quantum Reports
P.N.L.R.	Professional Negligence and Liability Reports
R.P.C.	Reports of Patent, Design and Trade Mark Cases
S.C.	Session Cases
S.C. (HL)	Session Cases (House of Lords)
The Times	The Times Law Reports
W.L.R.	Weekly Law Reports

Table of Cases

Table of Statutes

Table of Statutory Instruments

Table of Civil Procedure Rules

Table of Treaties and Conventions

CHAPTER 1
Admissibility

First thing's first: when can a party call expert evidence? Unfortunately, the 1.001
answer to this question is still not without uncertainty.

English law is unusual in that the parties themselves call the evidence. The
admissibility of expert evidence is derived from s.3 Civil Evidence Act 1972:
where a person is called as a witness in any civil proceedings, his opinion, on
any relevant matter on which he is qualified to give expert evidence, shall be
admissible in evidence.

At the lowest threshold expert evidence is admissible under s.3 "in any case
where the court accepts that there exists a recognised expertise governed by
recognised standards and rules of conduct capable of influencing the court's
decision on the issues which it has to decide" (*Barings plc v. Coopers & Lybrand*
(see below)). However, the judge in this case also held that expert evidence "was
not automatically admissible solely by virtue of its coming within section 3. It
must also be *helpful* to the court in arriving at its conclusions".

Indeed, the whole thrust of the CPR is that expert evidence will only be
allowed if it is really needed. In addition to the admissibility test, the Court of
Appeal (*Mann v. Messrs Chetty and Patel* (see below)) has set three further
hurdles which expert evidence must clear: a cogency test, a usefulness test and
a proportionality test.

As the Chancery Guide puts it (paragraph 4.7):   1.002

> "The key question now in relation to expert evidence is the question as to
> what added value such evidence will provide to the court in its determina-
> tion of a given case."

Experts and solicitors must now be clear about what exactly they are hoping
their expert evidence will prove.

Hurd v. Stirling Group plc (May 26, 1999) unreported

In this case the Court of Appeal (Swinton-Thomas and Tuckey L.JJ.) held 1.003
that a trial judge was correct to rule the claimant's expert evidence inadmissible
because its probative value added no further information in support of her case.

The claimant had worked for the defendant as a machinist in their factory for
16 years. On the day of the accident, as she had done many times before, she
intended to pass through a pair of flexible plastic swing doors. The right-hand
door was open as she approached, but it swung back towards her, her right foot
was caught under it, and she fell. There was some dispute between the parties
on the construction and working of the doors. The claimant argued the door
closed too quickly and strongly.

At the trial, the claimant sought to adduce the evidence of an expert, Mr
Salins from Strange Strange & Gardner, on the issue of how quickly the door

closed. His report, dated three months after his inspection at the factory (two years after the accident), recorded closing times for doors other than those causing the accident. The judge upheld the defendant's objection to the admissibility of the evidence:

> "... the time speed of the other doors some two years later in 1998 is not probative of the speed of the doors at the time in question which, apart from anything else, were according to the plaintiff used a great deal more than those which were tested."

The Court of Appeal upheld the judge's decision. Tuckley L.J. said that the judge was only obliged to hear relevant evidence: "Irrelevant evidence is inadmissible". He also commented:

> "The courts have shown an increasing reluctance to hear expert evidence of the kind that Mr Salins was proposing to give. This was not expert evidence in any real sense and the judge was entitled to take the view that the timing which Mr Salins had made of another door, (which was only an approximate) was not going to help him to determine the issue he had to decide."

The Court of Appeal then said that even if the judge *had* admitted the evidence, it was clear that he would have attached little or no weight to it for the reasons which he gave for excluding it.

1.004   **Comment:**   This, as one of the first reported cases on the admissibility of expert evidence after the introduction of the CPR, is a good example of how a judge is entitled to reject expert evidence if he does not believe that it will influence his decision or be helpful to him in arriving at his conclusions on the case.

Yates v. Simpkin Machin & Co Ltd (September 3, 1999) New Law 200069801

1.005   In this case the court considered the admissibility of evidence in personal injury matters.

The main claim was for damages for personal injury caused by exposure to asbestos. Applications were made by the four defendants for various orders in the Central County Court in front of H.H.J. Green Q.C. One of the applications was that the claimant be refused permission to rely on three reports prepared by an engineer, a psychiatrist and a nursing care expert.

The defendant said that the engineer's report dealing with exposure to asbestos was quite unnecessary. It alleged that the claimant should prove by his own evidence that he had been exposed to asbestos. If that were proved, it would be admitted that the exposure was negligent. The judge said that if the defendants really thought that the expert's report was unnecessary, their remedy was either to admit liability or to come up with some watertight formula upon which the claimant could rely. The judge gave the following example of such a formula: "we will not submit that expert evidence is a necessary ingredient for proof of exposure on the facts of this case". Short of some such formula, the judge did not see why the claimant should take the risk of ambush.

As to the psychiatrist's report, the defendant argued that the judge did not need a psychiatrist to tell him that this sort of physical injury would cause shock and depression in a claimant. The judge disagreed in relation to the point about depression, but agreed as regarded shock. The important factor here was that the judge read the report as diagnosing mild clinical depression which he considered was a matter for expert evidence. In contrast, the defendants had read the psychiatrist's report as referring to non-clinical depression. The judge considered that if this were correct, he might have agreed with the defendant. It was, however, open to the defendants to confirm this by questioning the doctor before trial under the CPR and this had not been done.

In relation to the nursing care report, the defendant argued that providing expert evidence in this context was unnecessary. The judge was of the view that the defendant should have admitted the items of debt liability and then complained that the report was unnecessary. However, the defendant had chosen not to make any such admission.

On that basis, Judge Green Q.C. held that the claimant could rely on all three reports at the trial.

Comment: This case provides guidance as to how judges should approach the admissibility of expert reports following the CPR. In this assessment, it is suggested that the court should take into account the parties' approach to the case and their readiness to admit facts.   1.006

Prosser v. Castle Sanderson Solicitors (April 18, 2000) **unreported**

In this case the Court of Appeal (Mance and Hale L.JJ.) held that the judge   1.007
should have acceded to the claimant's application to adduce further expert evidence, where the experts had reserved the right to reconsider their evidence. (The Court of Appeal also made some interesting comments on the form of the expert reports and the manner in which the experts' instructions had been given — these are covered in the section below entitled "Content, form and purpose of expert reports".)

The claimant was a property developer and claimed damages for alleged professional negligence by the defendant. The alleged negligence related to inappropriate advice given by the defendant to the claimant at a creditors' meeting in March 1990. In effect, the claimant complained that he was advised at very short notice to agree to the liquidation of a company in which he had a shareholding interest of nearly 55 per cent.

The issue before the Court of Appeal was the admissibility of fresh expert evidence — a letter about the value of a property owned by the liquidated company from a Mr McNeil, a partner in Bramley's Independent Estate Agents. At a case management conference the judge had refused permission. The Court of Appeal said that it accepted the force of submissions made by counsel for the defendant, namely that the Court of Appeal should rarely interfere with decisions made by the judge during the course of case management, particularly only four weeks before trial. However, the Court of Appeal said that this case was in some respects "unusual".

The first unusual factor was that the letter which the claimant wished to adduce followed on from a report which was discussed at an experts' meeting in which the experts agreed that there were still a number of outstanding matters as to the correct basis of valuation of the property. The Court of Appeal noted that the reservations which the experts had introduced made clear that they were not necessarily satisfied that they had all the material documentation, and that the claimant had indicated shortly afterwards, through his solicitors, that he was not satisfied either. The Court of Appeal said that one would have expected both sides to pursue the issue of the experts' assumptions, particularly after a letter from the claimant's solicitors raising the claimant's concerns.

Further, the initial expert reports themselves made it very clear that if there was any further information or documentation bearing on the assumptions which the experts had identified, these should be produced and the experts should have the opportunity to reconsider their valuations.

The Court of Appeal said that, if one stood back and balanced the prejudice to the claimant against the prejudice to the defendants, and the prejudice to the overall fair trial of the action, it was plain that permission should be given to adduce the additional evidence.

However, the Court of Appeal also noted that the substance of the proposed evidence involved a change of case. This was an "unsatisfactory feature" of the way in which the matter came before the Court of Appeal. The court said that if a report is sought to be put forward which has significant implications for the pleaded case, it ought to be put forward in conjunction with an amended pleading.

1.008   **Comment:**   This case demonstrates that in some circumstances it may be in the interests of justice to overlook procedural indiscretions (see the case report under the section "Content, form and purpose of expert reports"), thereby admitting expert evidence which would otherwise not be heard. The decision of the Court of Appeal gives a useful indication of the test to be applied in this situation: the court considered a number of factors, including the extent to which the new evidence had been anticipated by the experts and any prejudice that would be caused to the respective parties.

Pride Valley Foods Ltd v. Hall & Partners (May 4, 2000) New Law 200058503

1.009   This action arose out of a fire which destroyed the claimant's factory. The claim was that the fire was caused by the defendant's negligence in failing to discharge its contractual duty of care as project manager of the project.

In the course of the hearing HH.J. Toulmin Q.C. received evidence from two fire experts, Mr Calleja and Dr Bland. The judge commented that he had been impressed by the extent to which they had been able to agree on important matters and that this meant they needed to be called only to give brief oral evidence.

The judge also heard expert evidence on project management from Mr Forbes-Bramble for the claimant and from Mr Warner for the defendant. In contrast, the expert evidence from the project managers was criticised by the judge.

The judge referred to the following authorities on the admissibility of expert evidence:

- *Midland Bank Trust Co. Ltd v. Hett Stubbs and Kemp* [1979] 1 Ch. 384;

- *Bown v. Gould & Swayne* [1996] P.N.L.R. 135;

- *Re Barings plc* [1999] 1 B.C.L.C. 433;

- *Pozzolanic Lytag v. Bryan Hobson Associates* [1998] 63 Con. L.R. 81;

- *United Bank of Kuwait v. Prudential Property Services* [1995] E.G.C.S. 190, CA; and

- *Sansom v. Metcalfe Hambleton* [1998] 26 E.G. 154.

The judge commented that the starting point for consideration of admissibility issues is the judgment of Oliver J. in the *Midland Bank Trust Co Ltd* case. Oliver J. said that evidence which really amounts to no more than an expression of opinion by a particular practitioner of what he would have done had he been placed hypothetically and without the benefit of hindsight in the position of the defendant is of little assistance to the court.

Relating these comments to the case before him, HH.J. Toulmin Q.C. made observations as to the value of expert evidence relating to project management. He expressed the view that what the defendant had agreed to do depended on the contracts with the claimant and not on expert evidence. Furthermore, the judge expressed the view that "there is an initial difficulty in accepting expert opinion evidence in relation to the duties of project managers". The basis for this is that there is no chartered or professional institution of project managers, nor a recognisable profession of project managers.

However, the judge had been persuaded by leading counsel that he should receive evidence, subject to questions of relevance, and deal with the issue of admissibility of the evidence in his final judgment. He therefore received an expert report of over 100 pages with another 100 pages of appendices from the expert witness for the claimant. The judge noted that the report dealt with a number of questions which were questions for the court, not questions for the experts. The report contained many expressions of opinion as to what the expert himself would have done in similar circumstances. The judge concluded that the report offended against the established basis on which experts should give evidence and that it provided "little or no assistance" to the court.

Comment: The judge's comments on the difficulty of "accepting" expert   1.010
opinion evidence from an expert who does not belong to a professional institution or a recognisable profession has raised comment from Evans-Lombe J. in *Barings plc v. Coopers & Lybrand (a firm)* (see below). In this case Evans-Lombe J. said that the judgment of HH.J. Toulmin Q.C. was not a decision that the expert evidence was not *admissible* under section 3, Civil Evidence Act 1972, but an indication that the judge, adopting the modern approach, had given it no weight. Evans-Lombe J. said that if certain parts of the judgment are read as meaning that for expert evidence to be admissible there must be a "recognisable profession", then it seemed to him that it is contrary to the decision in the *Bank of Kuwait* [1995] E.G.C.S. 190.

Nevertheless, the *Pride Valley* case is a useful reminder to experts not to usurp the role of the judge and to place any opinion carefully in the matrix of both the particular contract and general standards of the profession.

Hazelwood v. Narayan (May 12, 2000) unreported

1.011   In this case, the Court of Appeal (Morritt L.J. and Charles J.) took a strong line and dismissed the defendant's appeal against an order refusing its application that an additional expert should be instructed in connection with a boundary dispute.

The Court of Appeal referred to the fact that this was a second-tier appeal and was therefore subject to the more restrictive test for permission to appeal prescribed in CPR r.52.13. There was no point of principle or practice or other compelling reason which justified the grant of permission to appeal, nor was the case management decision of sufficient significance to justify the cost of an appeal. The Court of Appeal agreed with the judgment given in the directions hearing by Swinton-Thomas L.J. in March 2000 when he said the following:

> "The whole purpose in making orders restricting the extent of expert evidence and directing that, if possible, agreement between the experts should be reached, is to save the enormous expense that is involved by instructing a number of experts and having those experts available to give evidence in court. Mr and Mrs Narayan are not of necessity deprived of the availability of expertise. They are in a position to subpoena Mr Lewis [their first expert witness]. It is a hardship for a litigant to be deprived of expert evidence, but the court has to have in mind that it would be more unjust to Mr and Mrs Hazelwood in an ordinary case if Mrs Narayan, for example, were permitted to instruct a further expert".

The Court of Appeal also noted that expert witnesses are under a duty to help the court and that this duty overrides any obligations to the persons who instruct them.

1.012   **Comment:**   This is in line with other cases on second-tier appeals since the introduction of CPR r.52.13 where the courts have taken a similar hard-line approach — see *Re Scott* (August 31, 2000, New Law 2001017501); *Clark v. Perks* [2001] 1 W.L.R. 17; and *McNicholas Construction Co Ltd v. HM Customs & Excise*; *Jenkins v. BP Oil UK Ltd* [2000] 4 All E.R. 2. As this case demonstrates, experts and the parties instructing them should not expect any different treatment.

Mann v. Messrs Chetty and Patel (October 26, 2000) New Law 2001019201)

1.013   In this case, the Court of Appeal (Nourse and Hale L.JJ.) considered an appeal against a judge's refusal to grant permission to the claimant to adduce expert evidence.

The claimant had brought a professional negligence action against his solicitors following their non-attendance at the final hearing in his application for ancillary relief in divorce proceedings. He alleged that he would have secured a far larger sum but for the negligence of his solicitors in failing to obtain: (i) a valuation of the former matrimonial home; (ii) a valuation of the business; and (iii) a handwriting report in support of an allegation of forgery relating to the sale of shares. The judge at first instance refused permission to adduce expert evidence on these matters.

As a preliminary matter, in accordance with its usual practice, the Court of Appeal noted that case management decisions are not to be interfered with unless the judge has erred in principle or the result of his balancing exercise is plainly wrong.

The Court of Appeal then referred to the overriding objective of the CPR, and stated that controlling the issues and the evidence to be presented is an important part of the process.

The court has to make a judgment on three matters:

- how cogent the proposed expert evidence will be;

- how useful it will be in resolving any of the issues in the case; and

- how much it will cost, and the relationship of that cost to the sums at stake.

The Court of Appeal praised the judge since these were the matters that he considered. However, the Court of Appeal agreed that the issues would have been much clearer if the judge had dealt with each of the three proposed items of expert evidence separately.

Before considering the three proposed items of expert evidence, the Court of Appeal made some general comments.

As to the issue of usefulness, the Court of Appeal acknowledged that expert evidence may have been useful to the court in assessing any loss that the claimant might have suffered from the solicitor's failure to obtain evidence at the time. The expert evidence would have helped the court to assess what a court might have done had the case been properly fought in 1993.

As to the issue of proportionality, the only evidence before the judge as to the costs of the proposed expert evidence was contained in an affidavit filed very late in the day by the defendant's solicitor. This, in itself, did not create a good impression in front of the Court of Appeal. The Court of Appeal noted that it is "no easy matter" for a judge to assess proportionality without pre-judging the claimant's prospects of success. However, if the requirement in the CPR is to have any effect at all, the Court of Appeal said that the judge cannot simply ask how the proposed costs relate to the claimant's best case. The Court of Appeal said that the judge is entitled to take account of the broad ambit of the claimant's likely recovery. The Court of Appeal added that this was particularly so in a case such as this, where the trial judge will have to ask himself what the claimant would have been likely to achieve had his case been properly prepared and presented.

After making these general observations, the Court of Appeal considered each proposed item of expert evidence: valuation of the former matrimonial home; valuation of the business; and the handwriting experts.

As to the valuation of the former matrimonial home, the claimant wished to commission a retrospective valuation and "driving past the exterior" report which would cost around £200. The Court of Appeal said that the cost of such a valuation was not high, and saw no reason why it should not be done by a single joint expert. An important factor was the fact that its relevance in the context of the case as a whole was considerable. However, on the facts of the case, the Court of Appeal decided not to interfere with the judge's refusal to allow this evidence.

Regarding the valuation of the business, the certified accountant wrote that he would need accounts for the three years immediately preceding the valuation date, accounts for the year incorporating the valuation date, background information from the then proprietors, and confirmation of prevailing market forces. For this he would charge £1,200. The Court of Appeal said that it believed that the court seeking to second-guess in the year 2000 what a 1993 court would have done would not be able to carry out that task properly without some independent advice. However, the court said that there was no need for a detailed investigation. All that was necessary was a commentary on the opinions expressed in 1992. The Court of Appeal said that it was essential that this comparatively simple exercise was conducted by an accountant jointly instructed by the parties. The court also said that given the limited value of the information in the context of the case as a whole, it would be right for the court to set a limit to the time spent upon it.

As to the handwriting expert, the claimant wished to instruct a handwriting expert to examine signatures on a share certificate and to give an opinion at a cost of £400. The Court of Appeal held that this would only provide evidence on a small part of the jigsaw. For this reason, the Court of Appeal did not interfere with the judge's refusal of permission to adduce handwriting evidence.

In conclusion, the Court of Appeal allowed the appeal to the extent of permitting the very limited evidence indicated above.

1.014   **Comment:**   As well as giving some insight into how far the Court of Appeal will go in allowing appeals on the admissibility of expert evidence, this case is particularly interesting because of the comments Hale L.J. made in her judgment about proportionality. Experts and their instructing solicitors should make a concerted effort to prepare costs estimates with care and in good time, and should expect these costs to be assessed against the broad ambit of the likely recovery in the case (not the best case possible).

Sturton v. Sutherland Holdings plc (October 27, 2000) **unreported**

1.015   The Court of Appeal (Aldous, Brook and Mummery L.JJ.) held that, where a fallback case is advanced, the other party should be given leave to recall expert witnesses to deal with it.

The claim arose following the sale of two companies by the claimant to the defendant. The claimant argued that it was entitled to additional consideration following the delivery of accounts. The defendant counterclaimed for damages for breach of warranty.

Only the decision on the counterclaim was appealed. The defendant relied on a set of accounts. However, at trial, the defendant sought to rely on an amended set of accounts. Expert evidence had already been given by two witnesses during the hearing of the claimant's claim. The issue for the court was whether those witnesses should be recalled to deal with the counterclaim.

The Court of Appeal allowed the claimant's appeal. It held that, had the defendant wished to rely on a fallback case, it should have indicated that it would do so before the preparation of the evidence in this case. This would have enabled the claimant to decide whether it was necessary to instruct its experts to answer the case. The Court of Appeal noted that when the experts met they did not discuss this aspect of the case at all because the claimant's expert had no instructions.

Interestingly, the Court of Appeal also said that the principles in *Ladd v. Marshall* [1954] 1 W.L.R. 1489 did not apply to this case because "there had not really been a proper trial of the counterclaim at all because of the way it evolved in a muddled way on the first day of the trial". (In *Ladd v. Marshall*, Lord Denning stated that there were three criteria to consider where fresh evidence is sought to be introduced: firstly, it must be shown that the evidence could not have been obtained with reasonable diligence for use at the trial; secondly, the evidence must be such that, if given, it would probably have an important influence on the result of the case (though it need not be decisive); and, thirdly, the evidence must be apparently credible.)

In conclusion, the Court of Appeal held that it would be just to admit the further expert evidence. There were clearly issues of fact and law to be determined, and there ought to be a new trial of the counterclaim.

Comment: This case is an unusual example of an occasion where the courts will admit expert evidence, even if, *prima facie*, it is not consistent to admit such evidence in accordance with settled law, such as the principle in *Ladd v. Marshall*.   1.016

Barings plc v. Coopers & Lybrand (a firm) (2001) Lloyd's Rep. Bank 85   1.016a

Evans-Lombe J. makes interesting comments in this case about expert evidence on derivatives trading, while reviewing, more generally, the law on the admissibility of expert evidence.

The claimant applied to strike out the defendant's expert reports, which were directed to the question of whether employees and officers of the claimant ought to have become aware of Nick Leeson's unauthorised trading.

Evans-Lombe J. said that the test for whether expert evidence is to be received is a two-stage test. The first stage is whether the evidence is admissible as "expert evidence" for the purposes of s.3 Civil Evidence Act 1972 (the "1972 Act"). The second stage is whether the court should admit the evidence as being helpful to the court. The main issue in this case was the first stage of the test.

Evans-Lombe J. reviewed various authorities (including *Midland Bank Trust Company Limited v. Hett, Stubbs & Kemp* [1979] 1 Ch. 384 and *United Bank of Kuwait v. Prudential Property Services Ltd* [1995] E.G.C.S. 190). He came to the conclusion that they established the proposition that expert evidence is admissible under s.3 of the 1972 Act "in any case where the court accepts that there exists a recognised expertise governed by recognised standards and rules of conduct capable of influencing the court's decision on the issues which it has to decide".

The expert witness to be called must also satisfy the court that he has a sufficient familiarity with the expertise.

Evans-Lombe J. held that just as the Court of Appeal in the *Bank of Kuwait* case found that there was a body of expertise in relation to the management of lending banks, he was satisfied that there was a body of expertise in relation to the management of investment banks conducting the business of futures and derivatives trading. He also noted that no attempt was made to show that the experts did not have sufficient familiarity with the expertise. For these reasons, the evidence was admissible.

The reports could not be excluded at the second stage of the test either since they would be helpful to the court.

Finally, Evans-Lombe J. said that the objections of the claimant about inaccuracies and bias in the reports did not justify striking out any part of the report; objections could be tested in cross-examination.

1.017   **Comment:**   This is a helpful decision to those working in derivatives trading. There is now authority that courts will find expert evidence in this area useful. On the other hand, in order to avoid the problem highlighted by *Liverpool Roman Catholic Archdiocese and Trustees Inc v. Goldberg* (see below), instructing solicitors would be wise to avoid an expert known to the parties in a professional or personal context. The expert should also avoid giving evidence merely on what he would have done in the position of the claimant or defendant.

LHS Holdings Ltd v. Laporte plc [2001] E.W.C.A. Civ. 278, New Law 201023602

1.018   The Court of Appeal (Lord Woolf C.J., May and Jonathan Parker L.JJ.) dismissed in this case the need for expert evidence when it was directed to the very point which the court had to decide.

The parties had entered into a written agreement for the sale to LHS Holdings Ltd ("LHS") of the issued shares in various companies, which together formed the hygiene division of Laporte plc ("Laporte"). The agreement provided that the amount of the final consideration would be based on completion accounts and a completion statement to be produced by LHS. The completion accounts and the completion statement would, in turn, be based on up-to-date accounts of the subject companies, but with provision for adjustment. The agreement also provided that Laporte could, within 30 days after receipt of the draft completion accounts and completion statement, serve a "Dispute Notice" if it did not agree with the contents.

Once a Dispute Notice has been served, the agreement provided that the seller and the purchaser should use all reasonable endeavours to resolve any dispute. If they fail to do so by the expiry of 14 days after the date of receipt of the Dispute Notice, the seller or the purchaser may refer the dispute to an independent firm of chartered accountants agreed by the parties, or to the London office of an independent firm of chartered accountants nominated by the President of the Institute of Chartered Accountants in England and Wales.

Laporte served a Dispute Notice which was the subject of this case. The material part of the Dispute Notice read as follows:

> "Pursuant to the terms of Clause 5(C) we hereby give you notice that the Company disputes the terms and content of the draft Completion Accounts and Completion Statement prepared by [PWC], dated March 2, 1999. Details of the grounds of the dispute are set out in the schedule hereto which forms a part of this Dispute Notice and should be read alongside this letter."

In the accompanying schedule, the third column was headed "Reasons for Disagreement". In respect of eight of the listed items, there appeared in that column the rubric "UK GAAP override not appropriate/improperly applied".

LHS contended that the use of this rubric (the "UK GAAP rubric") did not comply with the requirement of clause 5(C) that a Dispute Notice must set out "reasonable details of the grounds for dispute".

One of the issues before the Court of Appeal was whether the expert evidence of two accountants should be admissible as to how an accountant would understand the Dispute Notice and the UK GAAP rubric.

The Court of Appeal held that Rattee J. was right to exclude expert evidence in this case. It said that no expert evidence was required to interpret the acronym "UK GAPP" — its meaning is commonly understood (Generally Accepted Accounting Principles applicable in the United Kingdom). Nor was the Dispute Notice framed in technical language. It therefore followed that there was no scope for expert evidence as to its meaning. Further, the court noted that the expert evidence on which LHS sought to rely was relevant only to the question whether the notice sets out "reasonable details of the grounds for dispute" for the purposes of clause 5(C), which was the very question which the court had to decide.

The Court of Appeal held that the Dispute Notice and the UK GAAP rubric were reasonable.

Comment: The Court of Appeal was in this case critical of the attempt   1.019
to introduce expert evidence. LHS's purpose in seeking to adduce its expert evidence was not to show that the words of the Dispute Notice had some special meaning to accountants, but to prove that those words, according to their ordinary meaning, were too generalised to constitute reasonable details in accordance with the requirement of clause 5(C). Given that the meaning of the words used was clear, whether they constituted reasonable details of the grounds for dispute was a matter for the court, unaided by the opinion of experts.

Baron v. Lovell [2000] P.I.Q.R. 20

This case is considered in the section below entitled "Timing and delay";   1.020
however, it also raises interesting issues relating to admissibility of evidence.

Owners of the ship "Pelopidas" v. Owners of the ship "TRSL Concord" (1999) 2 Lloyd's Rep 675

This case is considered in the section below entitled "Weighing up the evi-   1.021
dence (seamanship)"; however, it also raises interesting issues relating to the admissibility of evidence.

CHAPTER 2
Availability of experts

2.001　If oral expert evidence is to be given, the Court of Appeal has made it patently clear that it is the responsibility of the parties to ensure that their expert witnesses are available during the trial window or on the trial date. The unavailability of an expert will rarely constitute a reason for altering case management directions. Whilst this is only one of a number of factors to be taken into account when instructing an expert, the austere reactions from the Court of Appeal merit consideration on their own. (See also the section entitled "Considerations when identifying who should act as expert".) The Vice-Chancellor's Working Party draft Code of Guidance on Expert Evidence sensibly provides that "those instructing experts should inform them *promptly* whether attendance at trial will be required, and if so inform them of the date and venue fixed for the hearing of the case".

Matthews v. Tarmac Bricks and Tiles Limited (2000) C.I.L.L. 1597

2.002　This case before the Court of Appeal (the Master of the Rolls, Clarke and Mance L.JJ.) related to the approach to be taken in relation to availability of experts for trial.

The case concerned a claim for personal injury alleged to have been incurred in the course of the claimant's employment. The claimant relied on an informal report by his general practitioner and a report by a consultant orthopaedic surgeon, Mr Osborne. The defendant instructed a consultant orthopaedic surgeon, Mr Dunkerley, and a rheumatologist, Dr Calin.

At the hearing to fix the date of the trial, the claimant's consultant said that, if the judge fixed a date, he would make sure he was there. The defendant's approach was to supply the judge with a list of the dates upon which its two doctors would not be available. The judge wished to select the date of July 15, 1999. When the judge asked why the defendant's experts were not available on July 15, the defendant's counsel was not able to provide this information. The judge held that the experts were to make themselves available and set the trial date at July 15, 1999.

After the hearing, it was found that Mr Dunkerley was going on holiday at that time and that Dr Calin had been subpoenaed to attend the Wandsworth County Court on the very dates fixed for the hearing. The defendant's solicitor appealed the decision.

The Court of Appeal upheld in vigorous terms the judge's decision. The Court of Appeal condemned the defendant's solicitor's approach:

> "They were regarding it as the responsibility of the court to defer the hearing to a date which could, with convenience, be met by the doctors. It was apparently thought that all that was required was to tell the court the dates that the doctors had indicated would not be convenient and the court would thereupon find a date which would allow the case to be heard to meet their convenience".

The Court of Appeal emphasised that this approach was no longer appropriate because "courts cannot perform their duty of conducting cases justly if the preference for hearing dates of doctors are always given priority over all other considerations".

The Court of Appeal considered that the question of video evidence could have been explored by the defendant rather than proceeding with an appeal. The Court of Appeal did not accept the argument that this was not appropriate because of the expense that would have been incurred by video evidence.

This was to be preferred to vacating the date of the trial and incurring the greater expense of seeking to appeal. The Court of Appeal also suggested that it might have been possible to approach the Wandsworth County Court (where Dr Calin was due to give evidence on the same day) to ensure that his evidence was given at a time which would enable him also to give evidence at the Plymouth County Court for this case. The Court of Appeal was not impressed by the fact that no request was made to Mr Dunkerley to consider whether his holiday could be changed.

The Court of Appeal went on to consider whether this case could be tried justly without the calling of the defendant's experts. It found that it could. The reports of Mr Dunkerley and Dr Calin could be placed before the judge, although that would mean that they could not be cross-examined.

The defendant's counsel referred to CPR r.39.4 which states that "when the court sets a timetable for a trial... it will do so in consultation with the parties". The Court of Appeal said that it was clear that it was important that there should be co-operation between all those involved. On that basis, the court was to provide the parties with information which they reasonably required in order to come before the court and make sensible arrangements. The parties should try to agree on a date and, where agreement is not possible, should ensure that they make all the relevant information available to the court.

Comment: It is clear from this case that when attending a hearing to set   2.003
a trial date, it is not sufficient to have only the dates on which the expert witnesses are unavailable. Counsel and instructing solicitors also need to be prepared to discuss with the judge the expert witnesses' commitments and the extent to which those commitments can be moved.

There was also comment by the Court of Appeal in this case as to the attitude which the medical profession should adopt in pursuing its forensic role. In this context, the Court of Appeal emphasised that it was important that in cases where doctors are involved, as much notice as possible should be given for the dates of hearings. If parties wanted cases to be fixed for hearings in accordance with the dates which met their convenience, those dates must be fixed as early as possible. However, if where the court does co-operate with the parties by fixing a date early on, it is essential that it was appreciated that "whereas the court will take account of the important commitments of medical men, they cannot always meet those commitments in a way which will be satisfactory from the doctor's point of view". If doctors held themselves out as practising in the medical-legal field, they had to be prepared to arrange their affairs to meet the commitments of the courts where this was practical. The Court of Appeal hoped that "the message will be understood by both the medical profession and the legal profession".

Rollinson v. Kimberly Clark Ltd [1999] C.P.L.R. 581

2.004   This case before the Court of Appeal (Peter Gibson and Judge L.JJ.) related to the availability of experts at trial and to the considerations to be taken into account by a party when instructing an expert at a late stage in the proceedings.

The claim was for damages for personal injury sustained in the course of the claimant's employment. Liability for the accident, which took place when she was at work, was admitted. The outstanding issue was quantum. Proceedings began in July 1996. The appropriate schedule of loss and a lengthy and detailed medical report by a Mr Campbell dated May 27, 1996 were served on behalf of the claimant. There was substantial delay by the defendant in service of its disclosure list and expert evidence.

During 1997, the claimant was examined on behalf of the defendant by a Mr Gray, who eventually produced a number of reports. A limited exchange of medical evidence took place in May 1998. In January 1999, the defendant requested that the claimant be examined by another expert, a Professor Dickson. On February 19, 1999 the case was fixed by the listing officer for hearing on June 29 and 30, 1999. An issue was raised before him about the non-availability of both Mr Gray and Professor Dickson on those dates. On these dates, Professor Dickson would be sitting as a member of the Disciplinary Tribunal for the British Medical Council and Mr Gray was due to give evidence in Manchester. In addition, June 30, 1999, a Wednesday, was normally used by Mr Gray to comply with his commitments to the care of his patients. The defendant issued an application to vacate these dates, but this application was rejected.

The Court of Appeal agreed with the judge's decision. The Court of Appeal held as follows:

> "It is certainly no longer acceptable when a trial date is bound to be fairly imminent, for a solicitor to seek to instruct an expert witness without checking and discovering his availability, or proceed to instruct him when there is no reasonable prospect of his being available for another year. The check having been made on the expert's availability in the near future being in doubt, then a different expert should be instructed."

The Court of Appeal commented that the way in which the defendant had instructed Professor Dickson lacked the appropriate sense of urgency or omitted what should "now be regarded as elementary precautions." The Court of Appeal's position was that in relation to Mr Gray's attendance, there was insufficient evidence to support the conclusion that if his availability for June 29/30, 1999 had been fully tested at an appropriately early stage, arrangements could not have been made for his attendance by a reorganisation of his timetable. In addition, the Court of Appeal was not impressed by the fact that there appeared to have been no effort made to find alternative witnesses since the decision reached by the judge.

2.005   **Comment:** This case emphasises the elementary precautions to be taken when instructing experts and checking their availability, especially if this is late on in the trial procedure. Instructing solicitors should make sure that experts are available and, if not, make alternative arrangements and not rely on the lenience of the court to postpone trial dates. The case also underlines that experts may need to be more flexible in terms of the time that they make available to the court. In this case, the court expected Mr Gray to rearrange his timetable to provide for attendance at court even though he normally set aside Wednesdays to comply with his commitments to his patients rather than attendance at court.

CHAPTER 3
Considerations when identifying who should act as expert

3.001 Beyond securing the availability of expert witnesses to attend trial, there are a host of other considerations that must be addressed prior to the appointment of an expert. One such consideration is whether the parties should elect a single joint expert. This issue is dealt with below in the section entitled "Single joint experts".

In addition to those mentioned above, the Vice-Chancellor's Working Party draft Code of Guidance on Expert Evidence helpfully sets out some issues for consideration by those intending to appoint experts, including whether the expert has the experience, expertise and training appropriate to the value, complexity and importance of the case, and whether the expert will be able to produce a report and deal with questions and experts' discussions within a reasonable time and at a reasonable cost.

The cases heard since the introduction of the CPR have not yet dealt with these issues. The cases discussed below raise further issues for parties to consider: whether the expert is known to the instructing party or employed by them, and other factors which may give rise to accusations of bias. These last two considerations are particularly important given the impact of the Human Rights Act 1998 and the frequency of allegations by disgruntled parties that Article 6 of the European Convention on Human Rights (right to a fair trial) has been breached.

O'Toole v. Knowsley Metropolitan Borough Council (1999) Env. L.R. D29

3.002 In this case, Dyson J. considered what expert evidence was sufficient in relation to claims relating to statutory nuisance.

The appellant was complaining that the premises which she occupied as tenant of the respondent local authority were a statutory nuisance as defined by s.79(1)(a) Environmental Protection Act 1990 (the "1990 Act"). That is to say, the premises were in such a state "as to be prejudicial to health or a nuisance". The main defects were that there was rising damp in the walls, problems with floorboards and only trickle ventilation provided to the bathroom.

The appellant applied for an order against the local authority under s.82 of the 1990 Act to abate the alleged statutory nuisance and to prohibit its occurrence.

The expert witnesses called by the appellant were former environmental health officers, now acting as consultants. They were considered by the justices at the original hearing as being "sufficiently qualified and experienced to be regarded as expert witnesses in assessing and reporting on the condition of the premises". However, the justices were not prepared to accept their evidence relating to the health risk. They considered that the appellant had failed to discharge the evidential burden upon her to establish a *prima facie* case.

On appeal, counsel for the appellant submitted that the justices had misdirected themselves in rejecting the evidence of the environmental health officers as to the health implications of the disrepair.

Dyson J. accepted the appellant's submission and found that it was not necessary for the environmental health officers to possess medical qualifications in order to express an opinion as to whether or not the premises were prejudicial to health, as defined by s.79(1)(a) of the 1990 Act: "the environmental health officers possessed appropriate knowledge and expertise which the Justices did not have. By refusing to accept the evidence of those witnesses, the Justices substituted their own view on this issue which they were not entitled to do". The evidence of the two experienced and appropriately qualified environmental health officers should have been taken into account.

Comment: This shows that evidence as to possible health implications need   3.003
not necessarily be given by medical professionals, but can be given by other suitably qualified professionals such as, in this case, environmental health officers.

Field v. Leeds City Council (2000) 17 E.G. 165

This case before the Court of Appeal (Lord Woolf M.R., Waller and May   3.004
L.JJ.) considered whether, under the CPR, a person employed by a party to the litigation could give expert evidence.

The claimant was a tenant of the local authority and brought a claim for disrepair and alleged resulting personal injuries. The main issue between the parties was whether the disrepair was caused by rising damp or condensation. If it was condensation, then the council argued that the disrepair would not be due to its default, but, if it was rising damp, then the council could be responsible.

One of the directions made by the district judge was that an independent surveyor's report should be obtained by the defendant council, and that a discussion should take place between agreed experts. An issue arose before the district judge as to the identity of the expert who should give evidence on behalf of the council. The council wished to use a Mr Broadbent as an expert. Mr Broadbent was employed in the council's housing services claims investigation section, and had inspected the premises when the initial problems with the accommodation arose. The district judge considered that Mr Broadbent was unacceptable as an expert because he was employed by the council. On that basis, the council appealed.

The issue which the Court of Appeal had to consider was whether under the CPR it was appropriate for an expert to be called who was an employee of one of the parties.

The Court of Appeal was not prepared to accept that because Mr Broadbent was employed by the local council he should automatically be disqualified from giving evidence. It was clear that the trial judge had been anxious to "reflect the undoubted spirit of the CPR, Part 35 . . . in the best way that he could" and was influenced in his decision by the need for an expert to be a truly independent witness.

However, according to the Court of Appeal the way in which the judge should have dealt with this matter was to indicate that, on the information with which he had been provided, the judge could not assent to Mr Broadbent as a witness. He could then have left it to the council to satisfy him subsequently, if they could, that Mr Broadbent was capable of giving this evidence. If the council wished to use a witness such as Mr Broadbent, it was important that they show that he had full knowledge of the requirements of an expert to give evidence before the court, and that he was fully familiar with the need for objectivity. In this context, the Court of Appeal recommended that in similar cases, the authority concerned should provide some training for an employed person which they wished to use as an expert. The council could then point to this training to show that he had the necessary awareness of the difficult role of an expert.

The Court of Appeal went on to make some comments of a more general nature. Lord Woolf MR remarked:

> "The ideal way of disposing of issues such as that which arise in this case, is for one expert to be appointed by both sides. Clearly, someone in Mr Broadbent's position is not going to be acceptable by the other side. I would hope that procedures will be devised where claimants in cases such as this inform the authority of the expert whom they intend to engage so that the views of the authority can be taken into account. That could lead to single experts being appointed much more often than has happened in the past which is ideally to be desired."

3.005   **Comment:**   It is clear from this case that there is no overriding objection to a properly qualified person giving expert opinion as evidence because he is employed by one of the parties. However, the fact of his employment may affect the weight of the evidence. When trying to adduce evidence of an employed party the guidance of the court is clear: sufficient material should be in front of the court in order to enable it to give the relevant permission. This would include details on the proposed content of the report and the relevant qualification of the proposed expert.

It is also interesting to contrast this decision with the more recent comment of Evans-Lombe J. in *Liverpool Roman Catholic Archdiocese and Trustees Inc. v. Goldberg* that "justice must be seen to be done as well as done" (see case immediately below in this section).

Liverpool Roman Catholic Archdiocese and Trustees Inc v. Goldberg *The Times*, March 9, 2001

3.006   David Goldberg Q.C., a tax specialist, had given advice to the claimant with which the Inland Revenue later disagreed, and the claimant brought proceedings for professional negligence. The issue before Neuberger J. was whether he should rule that expert evidence given by a friend of the defendant should be excluded on the grounds of inadmissibility.

The claimant argued that the report of the expert witness was inadmissible for two reasons. First, it argued that the expert witness in question could not, as a matter of fact, be independent. Secondly, it argued that the evidence was inadmissible because the expert merely said what he would have done in the circumstances.

As to the first issue, the expert witness had known the defendant for more than 28 years; they were colleagues in the same chambers of barristers and were good friends. Neuberger J. reviewed the authorities where the courts had been at pains to emphasise the importance of an expert witness being independent.

He referred to the House of Lords case of *Whitehouse v. Jordan* [1981] 1 W.L.R. 246 and the famous case of the *Ikarian Reefer* [1993] 2 Lloyd's Rep. 68, and came to the following conclusion:

> "In my judgment the fact that Mr Flesch has had a close personal relationship, and a close professional relationship with the defendant in the sense that they have been friends and in the same chambers for a long time, does not mean as a matter of law, or even as a matter of fact, that Mr Flesch is incapable of fulfilling the functions described by Lord Wilberforce and Cresswell J. in *Whitehouse v. Jordan* and the *Ikarian Reefer*".

On this ground, therefore, the inadmissibility argument was rejected.

However, Neuberger J. did go on to point out the disadvantages of calling as an expert witness somebody with whom you have a close personal relationship. First, it "may well provide fertile cross-examination ground [as to the expert's possible bias]". Secondly, "the judge deciding the case may discount Mr Flesch's evidence altogether on this ground, or at least view it with very considerable care". Neuberger J. was impressed with the argument that there are many eminent Queen's Counsel specialising in revenue law who are not in the same chambers as the defendant. Equally, there are many members of the revenue Bar who have not been friends with the defendant or, at any rate, for as long a period as the expert witness instructed by him. The judge said:

> "It is a fair point that, on the face of it, subject to there being a good reason for specifically choosing Mr Flesch rather than somebody who was less well known to the defendant, the defendant's advisers may end up having selected an expert whose evidence the court will feel obliged, having heard his cross-examination on this issue, to discount in part or wholly on this ground alone".

As to the second ground of objection, that the expert witness was merely saying what he would have done in the circumstances, Neuberger J. noted the comments of Oliver J. in *Midland Bank Trust Co. Ltd v. Hett, Stubbs & Kemp* [1979] 1 Ch. 384. Neuberger J. said that it seemed that Oliver J. accepted that evidence of an expert as to what he would have done is not so much inadmissible, as of little assistance. He also noted that in *Bown v. Gould & Swayne* [1996] P.N.L.R. 130, Simon Brown L.J. went a little further in suggesting that evidence of what the expert would have done is of very little assistance. Neuberger J. also referred to the following cases:

- *Routestone Ltd v. Minories Finance Ltd* [1997] 1 E.G.L.R. 1232 — Jacob J. concluded that the effect of s.3 Civil Evidence Act was to permit expert witnesses to give their views on the point which ultimately the court was to decide;

- *Re Barings plc (No. 5)* [1999] 1 B.C.L.C. 433 — Jonathan Parker J. held that expert evidence from an eminent merchant banker as to whether another merchant banker had been incompetent for the purpose of company director disqualification proceedings was inadmissible;

- *Sansom v. Metcalfe Hambleton and Co.* [1998] 26 E.G. 154 — Butler-Sloss L.J. said that before finding a professional man guilty the court should receive evidence "from those within the same profession as to the standard expected on facts of the case and the failure of the professionally qualified man to measure up to that standard"; and

- *Matrix Securities Ltd v. Theodore Goddard* [1998] P.N.L.R. 290 — Lloyd J. made brief reference to the fact that the evidence of an expert witness as to what he would have done in the same chambers as the defendant barrister was helpful (in relation to practice, rather than pure legal advice).

Neuberger J. said that although he had considered the authorities, he came to the conclusion that the right course was to leave to the trial judge the decision of the admissibility of the expert report. He did say, however, that it was "fair to say that there is considerable force, in light of the authorities to which I have referred . . . that this evidence is inadmissible or unhelpful". He also said that the authorities were not clear in the sense that, even if he came to the conclusion that the evidence in the report was inadmissible, he could not be confident that the Court of Appeal would not take a different view. In this case, it was particularly relevant that the Court of Appeal might come to a different view since it was only a week before trial when the hearing took place.

Neuberger J. also made some interesting comments on the delay with which the claimant made its objections about the expert report. He said that the delay of 14 months was a "formidable point". He set out detailed and structured advice on what he considered to be the proper approach when considering an application to exclude expert evidence:

- first, if the expert evidence is said to be inadmissible, then that point should be raised as soon as possible;

- second, if the objection to expert evidence is raised early, the court should normally determine it, unless the court is satisfied that there is a real possibility that the trial judge will be in a better position to decide the point;

- third, if the objection is raised late, the court should be rather slower to determine it. However, that does not mean that the court should not determine the issue if it thinks that it is appropriate to do so;

- fourth, the court should be particularly slow to determine an application to exclude evidence when the application is made so late that the case is coming on for trial, rather than at the stage of preliminary case management;

- fifth, in principle, it seems that if there is real doubt as to whether or not expert evidence ought to be put in as admissible, the issue should be determined in favour of admissibility; and

- sixth, particularly bearing in mind the overriding requirement of the CPR, where it is clear that the evidence is likely to be very expensive and very time-consuming, it may be that even though the court has some residual doubt as to whether it is admissible or not, the court should grasp the nettle and exclude it.

Comment: This case highlights two grey areas relating to expert wit-   3.007
nesses: expert witnesses known to the parties and expert witnesses giving
evidence on what they would have done in a particular situation. The latter is a
particularly confused area. As Neuberger J. said, the case law in this area is not
"pellucid" and some Court of Appeal guidance on the subject would be
welcome.

Postscript: The trial judge to whom Neuberger J. stood over the issue of
admissibility has now considered the matter (*Liverpool Roman Catholic Arch-
diocesan Trust v. Goldberg*, July 7, 2001, New Law 2010712502).
  Evans-Lombe J. held that expert evidence from the friend and colleague of
the defendant was inadmissible.
  Evans-Lombe J. acknowledged that the evidence from the colleague of the
defendant qualified as that of an expert under s.3 of the Civil Evidence Act
1972. However, he said that in his judgment the court should disregard it on the
ground that the colleague was unable to fulfil the role of an expert because of
his close relationship with the defendant. On the colleague's comment in his
expert report that "I should say that my personal sympathies are engaged to a
greater degree than would probably be normal with an expert witness," the
judge said:

> "It seems to me that this admission rendered Mr Flesch's evidence
> unacceptable as the evidence of an expert on grounds of public policy that
> justice must be seen to be done as well as done".

Evans-Lombe J. concluded:
"Where it is demonstrated that there exists a relationship between the proposed expert and the party calling him which a reasonable observer might think
was capable of affecting the views of the expert so as to make them unduly
favourable to that party, his evidence should not be admitted however unbiased
the conclusions of the expert might probably be. The question is one of fact,
namely, the extent and nature of the relationship between the proposed witness
and the party."
  The lesson of this postscript is that parties should not appoint colleagues or
friends as their expert witnesses. Indeed, they should not appoint anybody that
the opposing party could claim has an unacceptable "relationship" with the
instructing party. Parties and experts will not wish the admissibility of their evidence to be left to chance as a "question of fact".

Smithkline Beecham plc v. Advertising Standards Authority [2001]   3.008
E.W.H.C. Admin. 6, New Law 201011103

This case is considered in the section below entitled "Human rights and
experts"; however, it also raises interesting issues relating to considerations
when instructing an expert.

CHAPTER 4

Content, form and purpose of expert reports

4.001 CPR r.35.5 provides that expert evidence must be given in a written report unless the court directs otherwise.

The new emphasis on the duty of experts to the court has also meant that certain requirements as to the form of reports must be strictly complied with. The most important changes are that an expert's report must include:

- a statement that the expert understands his duty to the court and has complied with that duty; and

- the material instructions on the basis of which the report was written.

Interestingly, although some of the cases about expert reports have discussed the form of the report and the need for reports to be non-selective, only one Court of Appeal decision (*Stevens v. Gullis* (see below)) has focused on these key issues. The lesson from this case is that a statement on the expert's duty to the court must always be included in the report, even if the expert has no connection with his instructing party.

Another new requirement is that the expert's report must be verified by a statement of truth. To date, there have been no cases discussing this requirement but it is anticipated that, in the near future, experts will be required to sign a more elaborate statement of truth, equivalent to those used in the Commercial Court.

Knight v. Sage Group plc (April 28, 1999) unreported

4.002 In this case the Court of Appeal (Evans and Sedley L.JJ.) considered the definition of "medical report" for the purposes of the CPR.

The appellant was employed by the defendants from September 1989 until December 1994 and issued a claim for damages for personal injury and resulting losses. The case originally came under the County Court Rules 1981. Under Order 6(5) of those rules a plaintiff in an action for personal injury was required to file, with his Particulars of Claim, a medical report and a statement of the special damages claimed. The appellant obtained three medical reports: a letter from her GP and two from psychiatric consultants. However, she only wished to adduce the GP report. The defendant applied to have the action struck out on the ground that the letter from the appellant's GP was insufficient to comply with the County Court Rules.

The direction which the original judge made was that the appellant should instead serve on the defendant's solicitors copies of the reports of the psychiatric consultants.

On appeal, the Court of Appeal held that the judge should not have made an order directing the appellant to produce the privileged psychiatric reports.

The Court of Appeal then considered what other order should have been made.

The report submitted by the appellant was in the form of a letter from her GP, Dr Morris. Dr Morris said that the appellant was her patient who:

> ". . . has asked me for a letter confirming the background details of her illness.
>
> This 33 year old lady has a protracted stress related and depressive illness which has not responded to treatments to date. She has been unable to work since November 8, 1993 and remains unable to work at the present time with no early prospect of return to work, as many of the difficulties continue to be active.
>
> One of the major stumbling blocks Ms Knight (the appellant) has had is that her illness was caused by a work related disciplinary procedure with her previous employers SAGE and she remains in dispute with SAGE at the present time.
>
> I hope this information is sufficient. If you need any further details please get in touch."

The Court of Appeal was of the view that this was not a medical report which fell within the definition required for the purposes of the CPR. The court was, however, prepared to accept this report as a preliminary report which was capable of satisfying the definition at least for the initial period of the proceedings. The Court of Appeal made an order under which the appellant would have three months to serve and file further medical evidence. It was left to her to decide whether or not to serve either or both of the two existing reports or to obtain further medical reports.

The Court of Appeal also considered whether a joint expert should be appointed in compliance with CPR r.35.7 and r.35.8. Since the defendant was unwilling to accede to this, the Court of Appeal decided not to make a direction that a joint expert be appointed. The Court of Appeal, however, anticipated that a judge to whom an application was made after the three-month period had elapsed would want to know whether the defendant had in fact been willing to co-operate or whether they had maintained their present attitude of not being prepared to agree to a joint medical expert being appointed.

Comment: This case is an interesting example of some leniency by the   4.003
Court of Appeal regarding the correct form for expert reports. However, it is likely that the attitude of the court was significantly coloured by the fact that the case was not originally started under the CPR. Indeed, the matter came before the Court of Appeal only two days after the CPR came into effect. It is unlikely that the Court of Appeal would now give any party such an extension of time to produce a CPR compliant expert report.

Bank of Credit and Commerce International S.A. v. Ali (No. 3) [1999] 4 All E.R. 83

This case is considered in more detail in the section below entitled "Weighing   4.004
up the evidence (employment)"; however, it also raises interesting issues relating to the content, form and purpose of expert reports.

An interesting side issue arising in the case was that of privilege. One of the questions which arose was whether there could be privilege in information furnished to an expert for the purpose of the preparation of his report.

Mr Langman, one of the experts, had referred in his expert report to individual employment case histories. These were based both on the witness statements provided and on information provided to the expert at interviews he conducted. When the defendant applied for production of the notes of the interviews, counsel for the employees claimed solicitor and client privilege.

Lightman J. held that no privilege attached to the notes. Moreover, Lightman J. considered that, in a case such as the present case, Mr Langman should have annexed his notes of interviews to his report. If he had not done so, the party whose expert he was should have volunteered such notes to the other party as soon as practicable. Indeed, the judge's view was that "the opposing party is entitled (as is the court) to know the factual premise on which an expert's report is based." This requirement was particularly relevant in this case where Mr Langman's reports were expressly based on the contents of the attendance notes. In addition, the employees were asked repeatedly in the course of their evidence what they had told Mr Langman and to explain discrepancies between their own evidence as to what they had told him and what Mr Langman recorded in his report. In this case, the notes when produced were a valuable aid in resolving that dispute as well as evaluating Mr Langman's expert evidence.

4.005   **Comment:**   In this case, Lightman J. adds further flesh to the requirements of CPR r.35.5 and the Practice Direction to Part 35 in the context of privilege. Since the introduction of the CPR, there has been some confusion about what is and what is not privileged in relation to an expert's report. It is true that the CPR are not clear on this point. CPR r.35.10(3) simply states that "the expert's report must state the substance of all material instructions, whether written or oral, on the basis of which the report was written". The rules do not address the issue of privilege in draft reports, reports made in a pre-litigation period or information given to an expert for the purpose of the preparation of his report.

Some helpful advice is included in the Vice-Chancellor's Working Party draft Code of Guidance on Expert Evidence. The distinction that should be made is between advice and work for the court:

> "Experts who are instructed by solicitors on behalf of their client to provide advice owe a duty to the client. Instructions to experts at that stage are privileged, as are advice and reports made before the start of legal proceedings.
>
> In the event that the matter proceeds to litigation, the expert's overriding duty is to the court. If the expert is asked to prepare a report for the purpose of, or to give evidence in court proceedings in accordance with Part 35, any advice given thereafter by the expert acting in an advisory capacity to a party, may be disclosable, if the court so orders."

The issue of information given to an expert to prepare a report has now been addressed by Lightman J. (However, it may still be difficult to decide whether materials provided to an expert form the "factual premise" on which an expert's report is based.) Unfortunately, since the questions were not in issue, Lightman

J. did not address in this case privilege in instructions, draft reports or reports made in a pre-litigation period. These issues will, no doubt, arise in cases in the near future.

Stevens v. Gullis [2000] 1 All E.R. 527

This case before the Court of Appeal (Lord Woolf M.R. and Brooke and   4.006
Robert Walker L.JJ.) centred upon the consequences, for an expert, in not complying with paragraph 1.2 of the Practice Direction to Part 35 which deals with specific information that must be included in an expert report.

The claimant was a builder who was claiming for work done and materials supplied to the defendant. The architect who supervised the work issued a final certificate in the amount claimed. The defendant counterclaimed under various heads including defective and incomplete work and delaying completion.

An order was made setting out the timetable for expert evidence. This timetable included: a joint meeting of experts to be held with a view to identifying the areas of agreement and/or disagreement; a joint memoranda of matters agreed and disagreed to be filed at court; and an exchange of expert reports. Undisclosed expert reports would not be permitted to be given in evidence at the trial. In November 1998 a joint meeting between the parties' experts took place. Mr Isaac, instructed on behalf of the defendant, refused to sign a joint memorandum of agreement prepared by the other experts pursuant to the court order.

In March 1999, it was ordered that Mr Isaac comply with the requirements of paragraph 1.2 of the Practice Direction. Paragraph 1.2 requires an expert report to:

"(1) give details of the expert's qualifications;
(2) give details of any literature or other material which the expert has relied on in making the report;
(3) say who carried out any test or experiment which the expert has used for the report and whether or not the test or experiment has been carried out under the expert's supervision;
(4) give the qualifications of the person who carried out any test or experiment;
(5) where there is a range of opinion of the matters dealt with in the report
    (i) summarise the range of opinion; and
    (ii) give reasons for his own opinion;
(6) contain a summary of the conclusions reached;
(7) contain a statement that the expert understands his duty to the court and has complied with that duty; and
(8) contain a statement setting out the substance of all material instructions (whether written or oral). The statement should summarise the facts and instructions given to the experts which are material to the opinions expressed in the report or upon which those opinions are based."

Mr Isaac did not comply with that order and a further application was made under paragraph 1.2 to have Mr Isaac comply with these requirements. At that time the judge had before him a letter written by Mr Isaac which included the following:

> "Relevant qualification is a BSc (Hons) Building Surveying. However, I have been involved with renovation and disabled grants in a professional capacity for over fifteen years, having been an associate of a Chartered Surveyors for six of those years, undertaking architectural designs, specification of remedial building rectification works, drawings, preparation of Bill of Quantities, site supervision, defect reports etc.
>
> Although I am not a qualified nor a practising architect, I have extensive experience in architectural design having taught computer aided design and auto CAD AEC (which is an architectural design package) at a number of colleges in South Wales. I have also prepared architectural drawings for large prestigious companies. I am able to, if required, submit copies of drawings so that they can be assessed for their architectural credibility."

The letter concluded that:

> "I submitted all reports to the best of my ability, and each report was a true and accurate account of the condition of the building at the time of the inspections".

The judge found that Mr Isaac had not complied with the order and in particular with paragraphs 1.2(7) and 1.2(8) of the Practice Direction. Specifically, the last sentence in the letter of Mr Isaac was not considered sufficient to comply with paragraph 1.2(7) of the Practice Direction. The judge was concerned that Mr Isaac had not set out the substance of these instructions, in view of suspicions that Mr Isaac was taking his instructions directly from the defendant. Although the judge understood that Mr Isaac's evidence was vital to the defendant's case, he still held that Mr Isaac should be disbarred from appearing for the defendant on the basis that he did not seem to appreciate what his functions as an expert witness were:

> "It is essential in a complicated case such as this that the court should have a competent expert dealing with the matters which are in issue between the defendant and third party. Mr Isaac, not having apparently understood his duty to the court and not having set out in his report that he understands it, is in my view a person whose evidence I should not encourage in the administration of justice."

The Court of Appeal upheld the judge's decision. Lord Woolf made it clear that in addition to the duty which an expert owed to a party, he was also under a duty to the court. The aim of the requirements of paragraph 1.2 was to focus the mind of an expert witness on what his responsibilities were so as to bring the action forward in accordance with the overriding principles of the CPR. If the requirements in this case had been met, the real issues in dispute between the parties would have been identified. Because of the way in which Mr Isaac responded to the experts' memorandum (*i.e.* did not sign it), that was not possible. Mr Isaac had demonstrated that he had no appreciation of those requirements.

Comment: The Court of Appeal was particularly concerned in this case   4.007
that an expert should be aware of his duties under the CPR and should exercise
these duties in accordance with the overriding principles of the CPR. Specifically, he should be clear from the outset as to his instructions so that he can set
them out in his report and show that his instructions have not prejudiced his
view.

Prosser v. Castle Sanderson Solicitors (April 18, 2000) unreported

This case is considered in more detail in the section above entitled "Admissi-   4.008
bility"; however, it also raises interesting issues relating to the content, form and
purpose of expert reports.

The claimant was a property developer and claimed damages for alleged professional negligence by the defendant. The alleged negligence related to inappropriate advice given by the defendant at a creditors' meeting.

The additional expert evidence which the claimant wished to introduce was
a letter from Mr McNeil, a partner in Bramley's Independent Estate Agents.

The first point made by the Court of Appeal (Mance and Hale L.JJ.) was that
this expert evidence was not in "proper form": it did not contain the appropriate statements regarding the expert's functions, and it did not recount relevant
instructions.

The Court of Appeal said that criticism could also be addressed at the documentation recording the outcome of two meetings between the two experts. The
meetings were recorded in agreed notes signed by the two experts, but these notes
did not identify the experts' instructions. Further, they did not identify the material which the experts were given. The Court of Appeal said that it was apparent
from the notes that the experts found themselves in a position where they had to
search for source material on certain points, presumably by approaching their
clients. The Court of Appeal also said that a good deal of the problems which faced
both the trial judge and the Court of Appeal, seemed to have arisen from the fact
that there was no proper statement of instructions and that the experts were left to
find out factual matters on their own. In conclusion, the Court of Appeal said that
it was an "unfortunate picture after the introduction of the new rules".

Nevertheless, in the event, balancing the prejudice to the claimant against the
prejudice to the defendant and the prejudice to the overall fair trial of the
action, the Court of Appeal allowed the additional evidence to be adduced.

Comment: Despite the ultimate outcome of the case, the comments of   4.009
the Court of Appeal draw attention to the importance of complying with the
procedural requirements regarding the form of expert reports.

As to the requirements regarding expert meetings, the CPR do not, in fact, lay
down protocols for their conduct or for the resulting documentation. However,
the Vice-Chancellor's Working Party draft Code of Guidance on Expert
Evidence contains guidance on meetings between experts. It states that the
parties, the lawyers and the experts should co-operate to produce concise
agendas for any discussion between experts which should:

- be circulated 28 days before the date fixed for discussion;
- be agreed seven days before the date fixed for discussion;

- consist of questions which are clearly stated and apply, where necessary, the correct legal test;

- consist of questions which, by their nature, are closed, that is to say, capable of being answered "yes" or "no"; and

- consist of questions which enable the experts to state their agreement or the reasons for their disagreement.

Another body which has produced guidance on meetings is the Clinical Disputes Forum, which drafted the Clinical Disputes Pre-action Protocol, and has produced some draft guidelines. As to the documentation of the conclusions of the expert meetings, the guidelines contain a detailed list of the matters which should be included in a post-meeting statement:

- a list of the agreed answers to the questions in the agenda;

- a list of the questions which have not been agreed;

- where possible, a summary of the reasons for non-agreement;

- an account of any agreed action which needs to be taken to resolve the outstanding questions; and

- a list of any further material questions identified by the experts.

Ensuring that expert evidence is obtained and presented in the proper way will no doubt result in more cogent expert reports, and decrease the likelihood that further evidence will need to be sought.

Royal & Sun Alliance Trust Co Ltd v. Healey & Baker (October 13, 2000) New Law 100109601

4.010   In this case before Hart J., the issue was whether the defendant surveyors owed any duty to the trustee bank or to the individual investors.

In addressing the claim, the judge considered expert and other evidence on the issue of whether or not a reasonably competent surveyor could have advised in February 1992 that the development in question would be "let up" at rents averaging £6.75 per square foot within approximately 18 months from practical completion of the development. Hart J. discussed at length in his judgment the expert evidence he received on these issues and was highly critical.

Before moving to his analysis of the expert evidence he received, it is perhaps interesting to note the judge's comparison of the expert evidence with the factual evidence received from local agents:

"I hope that the expert witnesses will forgive me if I say that to turn to the evidence of the local agents (which in fact was given first) gives me more pleasure. Each was amiable, knowledgeable, and anxious (as I perceived it) to give the best account he could of the atmosphere of the times. Each also had an obvious regard for the other's expertise, with the kind of qualifications and reservations which competitors in the same market for services typically have about each other's particular idiosyncrasies."

So what did the expert witnesses do wrong? The expert witness who received most criticism from the judge was the expert for the claimant, James W. Steevens. The main thrust of Mr Steevens' argument was that the defendant failed to take account of general economic indicators available in early 1992 and failed to take account of a specific problem of over-supply in comparable buildings. The judge noted, however, that Mr Steevens' evidence failed the test of cross-examination. The judge agreed with counsel for the defendant that Mr Steevens had been "extremely selective" in the material which he chose to highlight in his report as supportive of his thesis. Here is a list of the various points with which the judge took issue.

- Mr Steevens made a particular point that the Investment Property Databank Index ("IPD Index") showed a fall in the South East region of individual rents of 3.7 per cent in 1991 and 10.9 per cent in 1992, implying that the defendants should have been aware of that. The judge said: "what he did not make clear was that the IPD Index to which he was referring was a 1997 or 1998 edition. It was not a document to which [the defendant] could have referred in early 1992".   **4.011**

- Mr Steevens did not disclose in his report that his own firm's January 1992 Quarterly Property Review had contained a table based on the then-available IPD Index which showed rising industrial rents forecast for the period from the beginning of 1992, through to 1995, and no period during which the level of industrial rents had fallen in the past, or was expected to fall in the future.

- Mr Steevens also purported to quote from that review selected extracts designed to show that the economic outlook was then generally unfavourable. The judge said that the extracts were: "in fact highly selective, and by no means a fair summary of the overall tenor of the review".

- For evidence of over-supply of industrial units on the Medway City Estate, Mr Steevens relied in his report principally on a document called "The 1992 Employment Land Survey (Medway)", from which he extracted figures which he analysed as demonstrating that there would have been a vacancy rate of about 50 per cent after the completion of the concept developments. When pressed, he was unable to explain how he had derived this 50 per cent figure from the information presented. He was also unable to state for what purposes, and crucially when, the document had been compiled.

- Mr Steevens also considered evidence from a comparable riverside estate. Mr Steevens referred to reviews in December 1990 (£7.24 per sq. ft.), September 1991 (£7.04 per sq. ft.) and December 1991 (£6.72 per sq. ft.) as illustrating the pattern of dramatic decline. The judge noted: "Mr Steevens had, however, deliberately excluded from this picture another riverside review at September 1999 (No. 9) which was reported to have been at £7.53 per sq ft.".

- Mr Steevens also "resorted" to factual evidence of his own which was not foreshadowed in his initial report. He informed the judge that he had himself bought a unit at Riverside "before the over-supply became apparent" in 1989 or 1990. He had visited the estate every year and was thus in a position personally to confirm the situation of over-supply. The judge said that he found this evidence unconvincing.

Unsurprisingly, the judge concluded that: "given the criticisms which I have made of Mr Steevens' treatment of the data relied on, I do not consider that by themselves they illustrate a period of falling rent".

4.012   **Comment:**   This case is a clear reminder to experts that they should not be selective in the material they put forward to the court in their reports. To do so, they risk personal criticism in the judgment of the court.

Eagleson v. Liddell (Personal Representative of Pauline Pittard, deceased) [2001] E.W.C.A. Civ. 155, unreported

4.013   In dismissing an appeal from the judge's assessment of damages in a personal injury action, the Court of Appeal (Aldous, Robert Walker and Hale L.JJ.) said that it would have been helpful to have had counsel's calculations, in conjunction with those of the judge, of the precise basis of the past loss of earnings and future earnings of the claimant. Hale L.J. said: "It would have helped us even more to have in the bundle a copy of the report of Mr Halliday, dated February 10, 1999, the defendant's employment consultant".

4.014   **Comment:**   This is a useful reminder to ensure that expert reports are included in appeal bundles wherever necessary.

CHAPTER 5
Duties of experts

Concern was expressed in the Access to Justice Reports about experts' failures   5.001
to maintain their independence from the parties by whom they had been
instructed. CPR r.35.3 seeks to remedy this by stating clearly that an expert's
duty to the court overrides any obligations to the instructing party. It is also
anticipated that paragraph 1.1 of the Practice Direction to Part 35 may soon be
expanded to set out more explicitly the duties of expert witnesses.

The clearest statement to date of an expert's duties under the CPR is set out
in *Anglo Group plc v. Winther Brown & Co. Ltd* (see below). The judge in that
case devoted a significant part of his judgment to this subject, emphasising the
need for independence among expert witnesses.

A useful test of an expert's independence is whether equivalent instructions
from the opposing party would yield the same evidence. Where this is not the
case, the expert witness is usurping the role of the advocate. Ultimately, if an
expert witness fails in this duty, the court may rule that the instructing party
may not rely on that evidence.

Other duties of experts under the CPR are less obvious (*Kapadia v. Lambeth
London Borough Council* and *Lilly Icos LLC. v. Pfizer Limited* — see below)
and it can be expected that more will become apparent as the case law develops.

In re B (a minor) (Sexual Abuse: Expert's Report) [2000] 1 F.L.R. 871

This case before the Court of Appeal (Thorpe L.J. and Jonathan Parker J.)   5.002
makes it clear that the role of an expert to treat patients is not to be muddled
with the role of an expert instructed to report in family cases.

The proceedings related to contact proceedings between a father and his
daughter ("F"). The first contact order was made by consent in October 1998
and provided for unsupervised contact for four hours each Saturday. After only
two periods of unsupervised contact, allegations of sexual abuse of F during
contact visits were raised by the mother. The police and the social services carried out an investigation. The father was initially charged with offences of inde-
cency, but the criminal charges were then dropped a few months later. Shortly
before the prosecution was abandoned, F was referred by her GP to a local child
and adolescent consultant psychiatrist, Dr Bazeley-White. The purpose of the
medical reference was to enable Dr Bazeley-White to treat F for disturbance that
had been noted by her mother.

In May 1999, the father's solicitors wrote to the mother's solicitors seeking
reinstatement of contact. As no agreement could be reached, the father's solicitors issued an application. In consequence of the issue of the application, the
mother's solicitors wrote to Dr Bazeley-White requesting that she provide a
report. In the final sentence of their letter to her they stated, "we are sure that
you have all the details of the case and we would be very grateful if you could
prepare a report for us which would hopefully help support Mrs B in any
forthcoming proceedings". Dr Bazeley-White prepared the report in response

to that request. In that report, which detailed the therapeutic treatment carried out, Dr Bazeley-White included F's response to anatomically correct dolls used to depict sexual activity which had allegedly been carried out on her. She ended her report by expressing her opinion that F had plainly been sexually abused by her father and that there should be no unsupervised contact in the future.

F's father applied for leave to instruct an independent forensic expert. The judge refused that application and directed that Dr Bazeley-White be jointly instructed to prepare a further report.

The Court of Appeal did not agree with the judge's decision. In its view, "it ought to be elementary for any professional working in the family justice system that the role of the expert to treat is not to be muddled with the role of the expert to report". The Court of Appeal considered that the mother's solicitors should have seen that it was impossible for Dr Bazeley-White to make any forensic contribution to the litigation:

> "it was an error of judgement on their part to have instructed her to report. The letter that they wrote seeking a report ignores all guidance . . . as to the importance of ensuring that any instructions for a forensic report are impartial and, wherever possible, are joint and agreed with the other side. A unilateral appeal to an expert for a partial report is something which should have disappeared from the litigation scene many years ago".

Dr Bazeley-White's failure was in accepting instructions to prepare a forensic report in the matter:

> "She should have had the experience and the judgement to perceive that she was disqualified from making any forensic contribution by the nature of her medical reference and by the nature of the work that she had done in response to that reference".

The Court of Appeal considered that the deficiencies in Dr Bazeley-White's contribution could not be remedied by some sort of fresh start on joint instructions. This was simply unrealistic.

5.003   **Comment:**   This case makes it clear that an expert instructed for therapeutic purposes by one party is not in a position to provide expert evidence for the purpose of litigation and certainly not to become a joint expert for both parties.

Anglo Group plc v. Winther Brown & Co. Ltd (2000) 72 Con. L.R. 118

5.004   This case before Judge Toulmin Q.C. provides an interesting update on the 1993 case of the *Ikarian Reefer* [1993] 2 Lloyd's Rep. 68.

The action arose out of the delivery of a computer system purchased by the defendant in the original action. In December 1996, the defendant had consulted a firm called FMC when problems with the computer system became apparent. FMC advised the defendant to write an adversarial letter to the claimant, and advised generally on its claim against the claimant. When proceedings were commenced, the defendant instructed a Dr Salmon as its independent computer expert. Dr Salmon owned FMC.

Judge Toulmin Q.C. criticised Dr Salmon's lack of independence. Furthermore, Dr Salmon took a confrontational approach to the action. The judge commented that this was particularly surprising given the criticisms of FMC as expert by Judge Thornton Q.C. in *Gretton v. British Millerain Co Ltd* (unreported). Judge Toulmin Q.C. was obviously also influenced by Dr Salmon's article in the Autumn 1995 issue of *The Expert*, the journal of the Academy of Experts. In this article, Dr Salmon wrote: "An expert witness appointed under current procedure is under no duty to the court as an expert". Other factors also cast doubt on Dr Salmon's credibility as an expert witness: for example, Dr Salmon claimed that FMC had never lost a case but, in cross-examination, Dr Salmon admitted that he had only given evidence in court on two occasions. In conclusion, Judge Toulmin Q.C. said that he found that, "Dr Salmon failed to conduct himself in the manner to be expected of an expert witness".

The judge then dedicated several pages of his judgment to general comments on the issue of the duties of experts. The judge was at pains to emphasise the importance of experts acting at all stages as independent experts, whether in order to assist the parties in reaching a resolution of their disputes or in narrowing the issues in dispute. As the judge points out, following the CPR, dispute resolution may be achieved outside the court procedure by way of independent mediation or techniques of case management pioneered by the Technology and Construction Court such as: 5.005

- "without prejudice" meetings of experts;

- joint statements of experts setting out the matters on which they agree or disagree;

- early mutual evaluation; or

- the appointment of a single jointly appointed expert who may effectively resolve the technical issue or issues which are preventing the parties from settling their disputes.

Bearing this in mind the judge referred to the case of the *Ikarian Reefer* and said that the analysis of Cresswell J. in the *Ikarian Reefer* now needs to be extended in accordance with the CPR. He set out eight principles as follows:

- an expert witness should, at all stages in the procedure, on the basis of the evidence as he understands it, provide independent assistance to the court and the parties by way of objective unbiased opinion in relation to matters within his expertise. This applies as much to the initial meetings of experts as to evidence at trial. An expert witness should never assume the role of an advocate;

- the expert's evidence should normally be confined to technical matters on which the court will be assisted by receiving an explanation, or to evidence of common professional practice. The expert witness should not give evidence or opinions as to what the expert himself would have done in similar circumstances or otherwise seek to usurp the role of the judge;

- he should co-operate with the expert of the other party or parties in attempting to narrow the technical issues in dispute at the earliest possible stage of the procedure and to eliminate or place in context any peripheral issues. He should co-operate with the other expert(s) in attending without prejudice meetings as necessary and in seeking to find areas of agreement and to define precisely areas of disagreement to be set out in the joint statement of experts ordered by the court;

- the expert evidence presented to the court should be, and be seen to be, the independent product of the expert uninfluenced as to form or content by the exigencies of the litigation;

- the expert witness should state the facts or assumptions upon which his opinion is based. He should not omit to consider facts which could detract from his concluded opinion;

- an expert witness should make it clear when a particular question or issue falls outside his expertise;

- where an expert is of the opinion that his conclusions are based on inadequate factual information, he should say so explicitly; and

- an expert should be ready to reconsider his opinion, and, if appropriate, to change his mind when he has received new information or has considered the opinion of the other expert. He should do so at the earliest opportunity.

The judge then referred to the judgment of Lord Woolf MR in *Stevens v. Gullis* [2000] 1 All E.R. 527 (see above) where Lord Woolf held that the CPR underline the existing duty which an expert owes to the court as well as to the party which he represents.

5.006   The judge said that his eight-paragraph formulation is also consistent with the judgment of Laddie J. in the case of *Cala Homes (South) Limited v. Alfred McAlpine Homes East Limited* [1995] F.S:R. 818, where Laddie J. criticised a not dissimilar approach by an expert. Further, his formulation was consistent with the judgment of Pumfrey J. in *Cantor Fitzgerald v. Tradition UK Limited* ([2000] R.P.C. 95) where Pumfrey J. emphasised the particular importance of experts being scrupulously independent in highly technical matters like computer cases.

Interestingly, HH.J. Toulmin Q.C. also pointed out that a failure to take an independent approach is not in the interests of the clients who retain the experts. An expert taking a partisan approach, resulting in a failure to resolve before trial or at trial issues on which experts should agree, inflates the costs of resolving the dispute and may prevent the parties from resolving their disputes long before trial.

5.007   **Comment:**   This case provides an interesting update on the 1993 case of the *Ikarian Reefer*. That case concerned a dispute over an insurance claim following the sinking of the Ikarian Reefer. One of the issues in the case was how the on-board fire might have started, and, on this issue alone, the trial judge heard 32 days of expert evidence. In his judgment, Cresswell J. made several comments on the duties and responsibilities of expert witnesses:

- the expert must be, and appear to be, entirely independent;

- there should only be assistance on matters within the expert's expertise;

- any facts or assumptions upon which the expert's advice is based must be stated;

- the expert should make it clear when an issue falls outside his expertise;

- the expert should state that his opinion is provisional when he believes that there is insufficient data; and

- any change in the expert's opinion should be communicated to the court and the opposing side as soon as is possible.

On appeal, the Court of Appeal (Stuart-Smith, Farquharson and Evans L.JJ.) endorsed the analysis of Cresswell J., adding a few comments of its own. In relation to the opinions put forward by experts, the Court of Appeal considered that it is inevitable that experts will change their views in the light of the opinions of opposing experts and cross-examination, and this should not be frowned upon. Further, the Court of Appeal explained that, whilst an expert should be confined only to issues that fall within his expertise, there would be circumstances where an expert in one field should be permitted to opine on matters where that field overlaps with others.

Re H (children) (2000) Crim. L.R. 471

This was a sexual abuse case before the Court of Appeal (Thorpe and Mance L.JJ.) in which relevant comments were made in relation to the duties of experts in the collecting of forensic evidence for a local authority investigation.   5.008

The issue arose in the context of care proceedings. G's parents had separated in December 1997. G's mother began a relationship with NB in the summer of 1998. During the course of a contact visit, G told her father that she had been sexually interfered with by NB. Professional investigations were commenced at that point by a clinical nurse. During the course of her sessions with G, the nurse introduced anatomically correct dolls. There were no further investigative interviews, either by a social worker or by a woman police officer.

Care proceedings were commenced in March 1999. NB was not a party and he took no part in hearings, which included directions regarding release of police records and the joint instruction of an expert. NB was not brought into the proceedings until July 1999. At the pre-trial review and again at the beginning of the trial, NB applied for an adjournment on the ground that he required time in order to obtain his own expert evidence. The judge refused the application for adjournment and went on to find that G had been abused by NB.

There were various grounds of appeal. However, counsel for NB was particularly critical of the nurse's report and investigation. He stated that her work was hopelessly flawed in that she seemed never to have directed herself as to what it was that she was doing: "Was she doing an assessment? Was she carrying out a diagnostic interview? Was she carrying out therapeutic work with the child? If she was carrying out some sort of investigative procedure, her use of anatomically complete dolls was plainly contrary to all available guidelines." He also commented on her failure to record the exchange with the child or the duration of any of these interviews, which was absolutely contrary to good   5.009

practice. She also failed to follow up the child's assertion of abuse by asking the vitally important questions that might establish the circumstances in which the assault had taken place. Another area of criticism by NB's lawyers was that NB was forensically vulnerable, being drawn into the trial at a very late stage. All the expert evidence had been gathered by other parties before he arrived and he had no opportunity of calling any expert instructed on his behalf to put it into its proper perspective.

The Court of Appeal agreed. It should be clear that investigative interviews should be properly recorded and should abstain from leading questions. They should also not introduce anatomically complete dolls unless the circumstances exceptionally required it. The length of each interview should be carefully monitored and recorded and there must be clear written instructions defining the task of the expert. The expert must then make a clear written report discharging the instruction given. None of that was present in this case. The Court of Appeal was further not impressed by the local authority's defence of the nurse's work and was of the view that a social worker or woman police officer could have been involved.

Nevertheless, the Court of Appeal's final decision was that the judge was entitled to reach his conclusion and that the findings of sexual abuse should stand.

5.010   **Comment:**   The Court of Appeal commented that it was regrettable that the local authority did not perceive from the outset that if they were going to assert something against NB of such gravity then it was incumbent upon them to take the greatest care and to adopt the best practice regarding the experts they used. This was both in terms of investigation and in forensic preparation, in order to ensure that what could have been a very clear case was not weakened and marred by a departure from the guidelines. In this context, it was therefore "really important to have regard to the guidelines that are specifically there for the family justice system, namely the Cleveland Guidelines and the judgments of this court explaining the importance of rigour and investigation".

Kapadia v. Lambeth London Borough Council [2000] I.R.L.R. 699

5.011   The Court of Appeal (Sir Murray Stuart-Smith and Pill and Schiemann L.JJ.) held that a claimant who consented to a medical examination by the defendant's expert could not later veto disclosure of the report to the defendant.

The claimant was employed by the defendant until July 1997 when he was retired on grounds of ill-health. He subsequently presented a claim to the employment tribunal that he had been unfairly dismissed and discriminated against on the grounds of disability. Two medical reports were prepared on behalf of the claimant and the claimant consented to the defendant obtaining its own medical report by a doctor employed by the Kings Health Care NHS Trust. The claimant was examined and a report prepared, but the defendant's expert refused to hand over the report unless the claimant consented. The claimant would not consent unless he could first see the report.

In these circumstances no medical evidence was called on behalf of the defendant. The two expert witnesses were called on behalf of the claimant: Mr Revell, a consultant clinical psychologist, and Dr Namasivayam, a registered medical practitioner. They each gave detailed evidence both in writing and orally to the effect that the claimant did come within the appropriate definition in s.1 Disability Discrimination Act 1995, and that he had a disability. Since no evidence was called on behalf of the defendant, there was no direct challenge to the firm opinions which the expert witnesses expressed.

The Court of Appeal held that the expert evidence presented by the claimant   5.012
had been unchallenged and that there was no evidence to the contrary. Though there might be cases where a fact-finding tribunal could reject medical evidence (such as where instructions have not been clearly understood), this was not such a case. The employment tribunal was wrong to substitute, for the medical opinions, their own impression of the claimant formed in the course of the hearing which took place at least a year after the relevant date at which the claimant's medical state had to be considered. In the opinion of the Court of Appeal, the employment tribunal could not reasonably reject the expert opinions from the medical doctor and the consultant clinical psychologist which were before them.

However, on the basis of the information before the Court of Appeal, the defendant's medical expert's report should have been handed over to the defendant. By consenting to a medical examination, the claimant had consented to disclosure of the report of his examination. The court said that the expert should have disclosed the report. No further consent was required from the claimant. A practice under which a person who has agreed to be examined but then claimed a veto upon disclosure was not in the view of the Court of Appeal good practice and was "an impediment to the fair and expeditious conduct of litigation".

However, on the facts of the case, this did not affect the outcome of the appeal.

Comment: This case is interesting to experts for two reasons. First, they   5.013
should be aware that even if patients whom they examine do not wish their reports to be disclosed, once they have consented to that in the context of litigation, it is out of the hands of the patient and expert. The court will expect any report to be disclosed. The case is also reassuring for experts to the extent that the Court of Appeal has made it quite clear that employment tribunals should not substitute their own views for that of experts.

Lilly Icos LLC v. Pfizer Limited (2000) I.P.D. November 23089

In this case Jacob J. held that an alleged contract, under which an expert was   5.014
said to have agreed with one party that he would not act as an expert witness for the other party, was unenforceable.

In this intellectual property case the petitioner was to make a revocation application in respect of the respondent's "Viagra" patent. Pursuant to the court's directions, the respondent nominated, and told the petitioner that it had nominated, Dr Louis Ignarro as one of its proposed expert witnesses. This led to an application by the petitioner that the respondent should not be permitted to use this expert witness.

Interestingly, the first comment made by Jacob J. was on the delay between notification of the nomination of the expert witness on July 26, 2000, and the application by the petitioner on August 17, 2000. The judge said that the nearest he got to an explanation for the delay was that it took some time to get the documents together. He did not consider this to be satisfactory.

The documents in question were an initial contract of consultancy and a later document in which Dr Ignarro was invited to become a consultant to the petitioner. A fee for a consultancy was named but Dr Ignarro was not, in fact, ever consulted in relation to being an expert witness in this case. The nearest the petitioner came to consulting him was in a brief "meet and greet" meeting between the petitioner, its solicitor and Dr Ignarro. However, it was not suggested that anything about the action or the evidence was discussed on that occasion. Jacob J. said that he therefore wished to make it abundantly plain that there was no question of the claim that Dr Ignarro should not act for the respondent being based on any breach of confidence, legal professional privilege or the like. He had agreed to be a possible expert witness as part of his general consultancy and no more.

Jacob J. then found that e-mails passed between the petitioner and Dr Ignarro in which the petitioner released him from his obligations under the contract without fetter.

5.015   Most interestingly of all, Jacob J. held that if he was wrong about the petitioner releasing Dr Ignarro without fetter, the petitioner would have secured a contract with Dr Ignarro whereby he had agreed not to act as an expert witness for the other side. Jacob J. said that he would "unhesitatingly" say that such a contract would not be valid on the basis that it was contrary to public policy. An agreement that he should not give evidence to the court would be to say that the court should be deprived of potentially valuable material. Jacob J. referred to the case of *Harmony Shipping v. Saudi Europe Wine Limited* [1979] 1 W.L.R. 1380 in which Lord Denning said this:

> "If an expert could have his hands tied by being instructed by one side, it would be very easy for a rich client to consult each of the acknowledged experts in the field. Each expert might give an opinion adverse to the rich man — yet the rich man could say to each, 'your mouth is closed and you cannot give evidence in court against me'."

Jacob J. said that this could be adapted to the present case, where a rich client might simply bind a number of people not to give evidence without even finding out what their evidence was or was likely to be, thereby foreclosing the opportunities for the court to receive evidence.

Counsel for the petitioner sought to distinguish *Harmony Shipping* on the basis that in that case there was in fact no contract between the expert and the party that had first consulted him. Jacob J. said that he did not think that that was a significant distinction. He thought it quite plain that, if there had been a contract, the decision in *Harmony Shipping* would have gone exactly the same way.

5.016   Jacob J. said that even if he was wrong about the previous issues, there were logistical considerations in play. He said that it was quite clear that if Dr Ignarro was not to give evidence, the trial could not go ahead in a few months time, as planned. He added that it would be quite impossible for the respondent to find somebody of sufficient weight in a case of this importance at such a short notice and that the petitioner must have known that this was the position. He commented that he thought the application was essentially "frivolous".

Also of note was the fact that Jacob J. commented that Dr Ignarro would in any event be subject to the overriding duty to help the court on matters within his expertise, a duty that overrode his obligation to the respondent. It should not make any difference whether, in fact, he was called by the petitioner or by the respondent. For that reason, the respondent should be able to call its expert witness.

Comment: In this short judgment Jacob J. makes a number of interesting   5.017
and general points about the use of expert witnesses. Most importantly, he makes the point that parties cannot contract in such a way as to prevent the court receiving useful expert evidence.

Re RA & SA (Children) [2001] 1 F.L.R. 723

In this case, Wall J. in the Family Division commented on the inappropriate   5.018
instruction of a psychologist without the knowledge of the court or the opposing party.

This was a family matter where the father was making an application for contact in respect of his two children. During the proceedings, the father appended an expert report to his statement. The report commented on a video tape that the father had taken of his contact with the children. The court's permission had not been obtained for this report, nor had notice of the expert report been given to the mother or her solicitors. Further, documents in the proceedings had been sent to the expert in anonymised form.

One of the main issues before Wall J. was therefore: should an expert witness accept instructions in proceedings under the Children Act 1989, where documentation was provided to him in anonymised form and where he was not informed that the permission of the court had been obtained for him to report?

To begin, Wall J. criticised the fact that the clinical psychologist instructed by the father made no enquiry of the father's solicitors as to whether or not permission had been obtained from the court for him to report. This was particularly concerning in view of the fact that his letter of instruction made it patently clear that he was being asked to advise in the context of heavily contested proceedings.

Wall J. was sufficiently concerned by this to direct that the father's solicitors   5.019
file and serve a written explanation as to the circumstances in which the psychologist came to file a report in the proceedings. When Wall J. inquired, through his clerk, of how the psychologist came to accept anonymous instructions without inquiry as to whether or not permission had been given by the court, he was answered in the following terms:

> "I should say that it is not unusual for me to receive instructions which are not jointly agreed to prepare a paper based report. It is not unusual for me to only see the documents or have only a summary of the case or see a video without seeing the clients. Furthermore it is not uncommon for me to receive anonymised background information and, in particular with Asian families, for the names to be taken out at their request. I had previously prepared a paper based report for (Ms A, the father's solicitor) when she worked for another firm and saw nothing unusual in what she was asking. I had no idea that the instructions did not have the agreement of the

court. (Ms A) had a discussion with me on the telephone about my availability and costs and wanted a quotation to apply for authority to meet my
costs. She said she would need the Court's approval. However, it was of
concern to me that I had no background information. I telephoned Ms A
to request this information and explained to her that I could not make
comment on the issue of contact without this background information.
Ms A informed me that she had a draft being reviewed by the involved barrister and would supply this as soon as possible. There was nothing to suggest that the referral was unusual.

In all my dealings with solicitors I assume that what they request me to
do has the agreement of the Court and is within the law (if I did not have
that assumption, then I would have to hold a cynical view of the justice
system). If I was to explicitly ask whether solicitors had Court approval for
my involvement then it is likely that they would see me as questioning their
professional integrity and knowledge of the law and I would be seen as
being turgid, pedantic and offensive. I assume solicitors work with the
requirement of the Court and within the law. I am sure the Court appreci-
ates the level of trust that is expected and assumed in these matters. It
never occurred to me that Ms A did not have the Court's permission to
instruct me and I did not question whether the basis on which I was
instructed was acceptable to the Court. It would naturally be in my expectation that my preparation of a report to be placed before the Court as a
legal document would have the Court's approval. I accepted the instructions in good faith as I do in all my work with solicitors."

5.020   Wall J. said that he wished to make it clear that he did not doubt the psychologist's professional integrity. However, Wall J. said that he was in no doubt
that his response displayed an important misunderstanding of the role of the
expert witness and of the relationship between such witnesses and their
instructing solicitors. Wall J. said that it was important that expert witnesses
should always understand their role in the proceedings in clear terms. In particular, they must know the terms of the court order which defines their involvement, and the purpose for which they are being instructed. If that information
is not provided, expert witnesses must ask for it.

Wall J. then made some comments in relation to the expert's role in family
proceedings, in particular. He said that the essence of case management in proceedings relating to children is that the process should be transparent, and that
each party should know the case that party has to meet. When it comes to
expert evidence, the issues to be addressed should be identified at the earliest
possible stage in the proceedings. The briefs to be given to whatever expert or
experts are to be instructed can then be defined by the court and permission
given by the court for the relevant documentation to be disclosed. Wall J. said
that it was contrary to the approach to expert evidence which has developed
since the implementation of the Children Act 1989 (the "1989 Act"), that one
party, without notice to the other party or the court, should commission a
report from an expert about which neither the court nor the other party knows
anything. Further, expert witnesses asked to write reports for proceedings
under the 1989 Act need to know precisely what the court requires of them in

order that they can properly fulfil their obligations as experts to report fully and objectively to the court.

It is for this reason that Wall J. said that the psychologist seriously misunderstood the position when he said that he "assumed" his solicitors must have obtained the agreement of the court in what they requested him to do.

Wall J. said that it was also bad practice by solicitors to seek to avoid the need to seek the permission of the court to instruct an expert witness by providing information anonymously. Equally, it was bad practice for expert witnesses to accept anonymous instructions. Wall J. said that he was "very surprised" that the psychologist said that it is not uncommon for him to receive anonymised background information.

Comment: Wall J. was at great pains in this case to set out good practice   5.021
relating to the instruction of experts. The judge said that he recognised that the only consequence in the instant case was that the father's solicitors were personally liable for the expert's fees. However, he said the following: "I hope, however, that what I have set out above will help to discourage the practice where proceedings are in being of giving instructions to experts anonymously and without reference to the court". The vigorous comments of the judge may of course be due to the fact that the case concerned access to children.

Stevens v. Gullis [2000] 1 All E.R. 527

This case is considered in the section above entitled "Content, form and   5.022
purpose of expert reports"; however, it also raises interesting issues relating to the duties of experts since the expert did not include in his report a statement that he understood his duty to the court and had complied with that duty.

Royal & Sun Alliance Trust Co Ltd v. Healey & Baker (October 13, 2000) New Law 100109601

This case is considered in the section above entitled "Content, form and   5.023
purpose of expert reports"; however, it also raises interesting issues relating to the duties of experts since the expert in this case was selective in the material he put in his report, and thus in breach of his overriding duty to the court.

CHAPTER 6
Human rights

6.001   The Human Rights Act 1998, which came into force on October 2, 2000 has a potentially significant impact on the rules governing expert evidence.

First, under CPR r.35.4, the court has total control over the use of expert evidence and should limit such evidence to that which is necessary to resolve the proceedings justly. This power lends itself to allegations that Article 6 of the European Convention on Human Rights has been breached, in that evidential restrictions have denied a party a fair trial.

Second, it could be argued that the appointment of a single joint expert is an infringement of parties' rights to a fair trial, although this has yet to be tested.

Third, there has been discussion about whether without prejudice expert meetings under CPR r.35.12 could be challenged on the basis of Article 6. This, also, has yet to be tested.

It is therefore surprising that more challenges have not been made to Part 35 on the basis of Article 6. This is perhaps because the one attempt to do so was firmly rejected by Lord Woolf himself in *Daniels v. Walker* (reported in the section below entitled "Single joint experts"). In fact, as the cases reported below demonstrate, at the time of writing, the biggest impact the 1998 Act has had on expert witnesses is in relation to bias issues. These occur where there is reason to believe that an expert may be biased towards one party. As the cases demonstrate, the result of successful allegations could be that evidence is excluded, or given less weight. Either way, it is likely to damage a party's case, and steps should be taken to avoid any hint of bias.

Director General of Fair Trading v. Proprietary Association of Great Britain [2001] 1 W.L.R. 700

6.002   This case before the Court of Appeal (Lord Phillips M.R., Brook and Robert Walker L.JJ.) essentially concerns human rights and bias issues relating to the judiciary. However, it has been applied in *Smithkline Beecham v. Advertising Standards Authority* (see below) in relation to experts, and it is therefore worth noting the reasoning of the Court of Appeal.

In October 2000, the Restrictive Practices Court began the trial of a contested application by the Director General of Fair Trading to discharge an order made by the court in 1970 exempting branded medicaments from the Director General's statutory ban on resale price maintenance. Two trade associations representing large numbers of manufacturers and retailers of brand medicaments contested the case as respondents. (Although the Restrictive Trade Practices Court was abolished by s.1(a) and (b) Competition Act 1998 as from March 1, 2000, s.74 of that Act provided that the abolition did not affect an application to the court which had not been determined by March 1, 2000.)

The members of the Restrictive Trade Practices Court on this occasion were a presiding judge, (Lightman J.) and, since the application raised issues of accountancy and economics, Mr James Scott (an accountant) and Dr Penelope Rowlatt (an economist).

In the course of the hearing the respondents applied for one of the members of the court — Dr Rowlatt — to recuse herself on the basis of apparent bias and for the whole court to recuse itself as a consequence of Dr Rowlatt's bias.

During the trial Dr Rowlatt had applied to work for an economic consultancy whose managing director was an expert witness for the Director General of Fair Trading. She issued the following personal statement two working days after she made the inquiry at the economic consultancy: 6.003

> "I have worked for some two and half years for Europe Economics, an economics consultancy. Many months ago I gave consideration to moving to another consultancy because I was unhappy where I was. On Friday the 3rd November, 2000 I decided to ring Frontier Economics to ask that firm if they would consider me for a part-time post. Although I had known earlier that Mr Zoltan Biro of that firm was an expert witness [on behalf of the Director General] in the Medicaments case, I did not recall this fact at the time: if I had, I would not have telephoned. I spoke to the personal assistant to the Managing Director to ask if I could be considered, and she said that she would telephone back. I asked her who were the directors of that company — she mentioned the name of Mr Zoltan Biro. After I had rang off, I realised that this might be of some significance and I decided to inform Mr Justice Lightman at the first opportunity. The first opportunity was this morning and he advised me to send this statement to Counsel for both sides. I have as yet received no reply from Frontier Economics. Mr Justice Lightman also advised me to send (and I have sent) a fax to Frontier Economics in the following terms:
>
>> 'In view of the involvement of myself as part of the Court and Mr Biro as an expert witness in the Medicaments case, the application which I made to the personal assistant to the Managing Director cannot be pursued until after the conclusion of the trial'."

Two days after counsel for the appellants invited Dr Rowlatt to recuse herself from sitting further in the case, Dr Rowlatt sent a further fax to the parties which included the following: 6.004

> "As soon as I appreciated that Frontier Economics was instructed by the respondents in this case, I realised that it would be inappropriate for me to join that firm, and it is now clear that Frontier Economics has no interest in my joining them. To confirm my position, I would be happy to give an undertaking not to join that firm for two years after the final order in these proceedings or indeed for any lengthier period which either party may request. I have no regret in withdrawing the application. If I had had in mind the involvement of Frontier Economics in the case, I would never have made the application in the first place.
>
> I am confident that I retain (as I have retained throughout this whole case) the essential independence of mind required as a member of the Court and (unless persuaded to the contrary by the submissions made by

the respondents on their application to the Court) I do not consider that I
ought to recuse myself."

The Restrictive Practice Court refused the application that Dr Rowlatt and the
rest of the court should recuse themselves. However, the Court of Appeal disagreed.

6.005   The Court of Appeal said that the substantive decision to be made in this
case was one in which the public interest is paramount. It would be quite
wrong to treat the issue of bias as if it were simply a point of contention in
litigation between two parties. The court referred to Article 6 of the European
Convention on Human Rights, which includes a requirement that a tribunal
should be independent and impartial. The Court of Appeal also took the
opportunity to review the case of *R v. Gough* [1993] A.C. 646 which sets out
the existing test for bias under English common law to see whether the test is
in conflict with the jurisprudence of the European Court of Human Rights.
The Court of Appeal summarised the House of Lords' approach in *Gough* as
follows:

- the reviewing court should first identify all the circumstances that are
  relevant to the issue of bias;

- the reviewing court should not then consider the effect that those circumstances would have upon a reasonable observer; rather

- the reviewing court should itself decide whether, in the light of the relevant circumstances, there was a real danger that the inferior tribunal was
  biased.

The Court of Appeal held that when the Strasbourg jurisprudence is taken
into account, it believed that a modest adjustment of the test in *Gough* is called
for, which makes it plain that it is, in effect, no different from the test applied in
most of the Commonwealth and in Scotland. The test is as follows: the court
must first ascertain all the circumstances which have a bearing on the suggestion
that the judge was biased. It must then ask whether those circumstances would
lead a fair-minded and informed observer to conclude that there was a real possibility, or a real danger, that the tribunal was biased.

6.006   In this case, the Court of Appeal said that it was not appropriate that the
court below should have set out to answer the question of whether or not Dr
Rowlatt's statement was truthful. The court should have considered what
impression her conduct, including her explanation for it, would have had on a
fair-minded observer. The Court of Appeal, for its part, did not consider that
the reasoning of the court would have left the fair-minded observer confident
that Dr Rowlatt had forgotten about the economic consultancy's role as experts
in the case when she applied for a post with them.

The Court of Appeal considered that the fair-minded observer would be concerned that, if Dr Rowlatt esteemed the economic consultancy sufficiently to
wish to be employed by them, she might consciously or unconsciously be
inclined to consider them a more reliable source of expert opinion than their
rivals. The court also said that the fair-minded observer would not be convinced
that all prospects of Dr Rowlatt working for the economic consultancy at some

time in the future had been destroyed, nor that she might not still hope, in due course, to work for the economic consultancy.

It was for these reasons that the Court of Appeal concluded that a fair-minded observer would apprehend that there was a real danger that Dr Rowlatt would be unable to make an objective and impartial appraisal of the expert evidence placed before the court by the relevant economic consultancy. On objection being taken, she should have recused herself.

Further, having reached that decision, the Court of Appeal then had to consider the position of the other two members of the court. It held that the trial had reached an advanced stage by the time it was interrupted by the appellant's application, and that Dr Rowlatt must have discussed the economic issues with the other members of the court. The Court of Appeal therefore concluded that it was inevitable that the decision that Dr Rowlatt should be disqualified carried with it a consequence that the other two members of the court should also stand down.

The Court of Appeal said that they reached their decision with some regret since its consequence was that an immense amount of industry would be wasted and very substantial costs thrown away.

Interestingly, the postscript to the judgment records that while the Court of Appeal was preparing the judgment, it came to the attention of the Master of the Rolls that Dr Rowlatt was known to him, although only by sight, because she is a near neighbour. The Court of Appeal said that while this was not a fact which could cast doubt on the objectivity with which the court addressed the issues in the case, it was right that it should be recorded!

Comment: This case is a salient warning to experts dealing with the judi-   6.007
ciary: if experts have contact with the judiciary, they risk upsetting their clients with an application that the relevant judge should recuse himself or herself. The decision of the Court of Appeal that the judge should recuse herself is quite striking. Although the Court of Appeal described the set of facts in this case as "*remarkable*", it is arguable that the member of the court in question behaved in as proper a fashion as was possible in the circumstances.

Smithkline Beecham plc v. Advertising Standards Authority [2001] E.W.H.C. Admin. 6, New Law 201011103

In this case, Hunt J. heard a challenge by the claimant against the decision   6.008
of the Council of the Advertising Standards Authority ("ASA") on their adjudication of three complaints about the claimant's soft drink called "Ribena ToothKind No Added Sugar".

The main thrust of the claimant's argument was that the ASA engaged as a consultant a Dr Creanor who, before he was engaged, had allied himself publicly with complaints about the claimant's advertising of Ribena ToothKind. The claimant said that it was unfair for the ASA to rely on Dr Creanor as an expert since he was not impartial, or at the very least, there were insufficient guarantees to exclude legitimate doubt about his impartiality. When he was first consulted by the ASA, Dr Creanor was asked "if he was biased in any way". Dr Creanor had responded that "he was carrying out his own research into the product out of professional interest". He asserted that he was totally impartial and would remain so. He made no reference to his publicised statements in support of a complaint about Ribena ToothKind. The claimant argued that the ASA would not have regarded Dr Creanor as impartial and appropriate had they known of his public statements before retaining him.

Hunt J. said that it was unfortunate that Dr Creanor did not disclose his comments and the press report to the ASA when asked on engagement about any association with the parties. However, Hunt J. said that it was plain that the Council of the ASA were well aware of these comments and of the claimant's criticisms of Dr Creanor before they came to their final decision. Importantly, the judge held that the Council treated Dr Creanor as one would expect a consultee to be treated (*i.e.* as an advisor and not a decision-maker). The judge elaborated by explaining that Dr Creanor was not in the position of a juror or a justice's clerk retiring with the tribunal to be part of the decision-making process. He was simply one factor in that process. The judge was also influenced by the fact that Dr Creanor's report was disclosed.

6.009   **Comment:**   This is an interesting case on expert evidence outside the courtroom. Although Dr Creanor is described throughout the judgment as a "consultee", Hunt J. does, later in his judgment, state that he was satisfied that the Council of the ASA had taken into account "all the expert views they received as well as their own". He also referred to "the totality of all the expert evidence including that relied on by [the claimant]".
Hunt J. concluded his judgment by stating:

> "In short, I find on examining all the relevant material that those circumstances would not lead a fair-minded and informed observer to conclude that there was a real danger of bias either in Dr Creanor or, and more particularly, in the ASA".

Previously, the test of fair-minded and informed observer had been applied to the judiciary only (*Director General of Fair Trading v. The Proprietary Association of Great Britain* — see above). However, it might be that we will see more applications of this test to expert witnesses when they are being used as consultees by tribunals or even to experts consulted for the purposes of litigation. In any event, the impact of the Human Rights Act 1998 will mean that challenges may be made to expert evidence on the ground that impartiality is a breach of Article 6.

Daniels v. Walker [2000] 1 W.L.R. 1382

6.010   This case is considered in the section below entitled "Single joint experts"; however, it also raises interesting issues relating to the Human Rights Act 1998.

CHAPTER 7
Immunity

The basic rule is that experts cannot be sued for work in court proceedings: 7.001
Stanton v. Callaghan [2000] 1 Q.B. 75. Some commentators have considered
whether the abolition of advocates' immunity in *Hall v. Simons* (2000) 3 W.L.R.
543 might have an effect on the court's approach to experts' immunity. Equally,
parties could argue that experts' immunity is contrary to Article 6 of the European Convention on Human Rights (right to a fair trial). However, the only case
concerning the immunity of experts since the introduction of the CPR does not
indicate any willingness on the part of the court to restrict the immunity of
experts.

Raiss v. Paimano [2001] P.N.L.R. 540

The issue before Eady J. in this case was the immunity from suit of an expert   7.002
witness in relation to a statement in his report and his performance under cross-
examination.

The claimant brought an action against the defendant, his former expert witness, for wasted costs and losses caused by the defendant's negligent advice. The
defendant argued that the claim fell foul of the principle of witness immunity
from suit.

The defendant had been instructed by the claimant to advise him on the merits of his claim against a firm of surveyors. The defendant advised the claimant
that:

- he had considerable professional knowledge and experience in respect of
  properties in Covent Garden;

- he was the ideal person to advise the claimant and act as his expert witness in respect of his dispute with the surveyors in the County Court
  proceedings;

- he was on the Panel of Arbitrators to the R.I.C.S.; and

- the claimant had a good claim against the surveyors.

The defendant then produced an expert report for the purpose of the County
Court proceedings. The report stated, among other things:

> "Roger Paimano, B.A.(Hons), F.R.I.C.S., is a Fellow of the Royal Institu-
> tion of Chartered Surveyors and on the Panel of Arbitrators to the Institu-
> tion. He has been practising in London for 19 years and has extensive
> experience of open market property transactions in Central London."

During the course of the defendant's cross-examination at trial it became   7.003
apparent that:

- he was not, in fact, on the Panel of Arbitrators to the R.I.C.S.; and

- he was not an expert in respect of the Covent Garden area.

The Master hearing the claim drew a distinction between the way the expert described his experience in relation to Covent Garden, which was insufficient to lift the expert witness immunity, and the deceitful statement concerning the defendant's qualification to which immunity should not attach.

Eady J. disagreed. He said that the distinction drawn by the Master could not be sustained in the terms in which he expressed it. In giving his judgment, Eady J. referred at length to the authorities on the immunity of expert witnesses, including the decision of the Court of Appeal in *Stanton v. Callaghan* [2000] 1 Q.B. 75. In this case Chadwick L.J. said:

> "What, then, is the position in relation to expert reports? It seems to me that the following propositions are supported by authority binding in this court: (i) an expert witness who gives evidence at a trial is immune from suit in respect of anything which he says in court, and that immunity will extend to the contents of the report which he adopts as, or incorporates in, his evidence; (ii) where an expert witness gives evidence at a trial the immunity which he would enjoy in respect of that evidence is not to be circumvented by a suit based on the report itself; and (iii) the immunity does not extend to protect an expert who has been retained to advise as to the merits of a party's claim in litigation from a suit by the party by whom he has been retained in respect of that advice, notwithstanding that it was in contemplation at the time when the advice was given that the expert would be a witness at the trial if that litigation were to proceed."

On the facts of this case, Eady J. agreed that the claimant's complaints on the defendant's performance under cross-examination should be struck out. In relation to the untrue statement in the report, Eady J. said that it was clear in the light of that authority that a witness is entitled to immunity for reasons of public policy even in respect of evidence that turns out to have been dishonest (House of Lords decision in *Darker v. Chief Constable of the West Midlands* [2000] 3 W.L.R. 747). Eady J. said: "although it may seem surprising as a matter of first impression, the immunity applies".

7.004   **Comment:**   This is an extremely interesting decision given the stress placed, under the CPR, on the duties of experts to the court. The case is clear authority for the fact that immunity applies even if an expert witness is dishonest.

However, it is important to note that Eady J. was of the view that the real issue in this case was the defendant's performance in the witness box, not pre-report representations. Experts should not forget that an expert will not necessarily be protected by immunity in relation to preliminary advice on the merits of proposed litigation or pre-report representations. Eady J. referred in this case to the decision of Mr Simon Tuckey Q.C. in *Palmer v. Dunford Ford* [1992] Q.B. 483 in which Mr Tuckey Q.C. said:

". . . immunity would only extend to what could fairly be said to be pre-liminary to his giving evidence in court judged perhaps, by the principal purpose for which the work was done. So the production or approval of a report for the purposes of disclosure to the other side would be immune but work done for the principal purpose of advising the client would not. Each case would depend upon its own facts with the court concerned to protect the expert from liability for the evidence which he gave in court and the work principally and proximately leading thereto."

This statement by Mr Tuckey Q.C. was cited by Otton L.J. in *Stanton* and considered in the Court of Appeal and the House of Lords without being in any way criticised.   7.005

At present, if the test of "principal and proximate connection" is satisfied, the pre-hearing work of an expert will also come within the protective circle of the witness immunity principle. It will be interesting to see whether this remains the case as the twin roles of experts as advisers and Part 35 witnesses become more entrenched and as our human rights jurisprudence develops.

CHAPTER 8
Limitation

8.001   The relevance of expert evidence in the context of limitation issues has been mainly concerned with the question of when the claimant is deemed to have sufficient knowledge for the purpose of the Limitation Act 1980. This question arises where the limitation period (within which a claim must be brought), instead of beginning when the claimant's cause of action accrues, only starts to run when the claimant has sufficient knowledge of his potential claim. Sometimes this knowledge is dependent on the advice of experts. In those circumstances, the cases heard since the introduction of the CPR have demonstrated that the limitation period will only start to run once expert evidence has been obtained (and not when the advice is sought) and that this will be the case regardless of whether the expert evidence obtained is favourable or not.

Ali v. Courtaulds Textiles Ltd [1999] Lloyd's Rep. Med. 301

8.002   This case before the Court of Appeal (Lord Henry L.J. and Holman J.) was concerned with the relevance of expert evidence when determining relevant knowledge for the purposes of the Limitation Act 1980 (the "1980 Act").

The claimant was in his sixties and had worked for some 20 years in two cotton mills owned by the defendant in Lancashire. The claimant complained of deafness to his GP in 1986 and again in September 1990. In November 1991, the claimant was told by a community worker that this sort of problem could be caused by working in a cotton mill and that he should consult a doctor and a solicitor. The claimant consulted solicitors the very next day. A legal aid certificate was obtained which was initially limited to the obtaining of a medical report. That report was completed in August 1992 and communicated to the claimant in September 1992. The report concluded that the claimant's hearing loss was more likely than not caused by exposure to industrial noise. Proceedings were commenced in May 1995 and the defendant raised a limitation defence. As a preliminary issue, the judge held that the action was time-barred because the claimant had relevant knowledge in November 1991 that his deafness was capable of being attributed to his exposure to noise in the mills.

The Court of Appeal considered at which time the claimant should be fixed with knowledge for the purposes of s.14 of the 1980 Act. It was clear to the Court of Appeal that the claimant knew as of September 1990 (date of the second visit of the claimant to his GP) that his injuries were significant. The active question, however, was at which time the claimant first had knowledge of the fact that his deafness was attributable to his employer's failure to provide proper protection against the noise in the mills.

The Court of Appeal considered, in particular, s.14(3) of the 1980 Act, which reads as follows:

"For the purposes of this section a person's knowledge includes knowledge that he might reasonably have been expected to acquire:

(a) from facts observable or ascertainable by him; or
(b) from facts ascertainable by him with the help of medical or other appropriate expert advice which it is reasonable for him to seek; but a person shall not be fixed under this sub-section with knowledge of a fact ascertainable only with the help of expert advice so long as he has taken all reasonable steps to obtain (and, where appropriate, act on) that advice."

The Court of Appeal's view was that, in this case, medical expertise was key to determining the question of whether deafness was caused by the ageing process or was caused by unprotected exposure to noise at work. For the purpose of s.14(3)(b) of the 1980 Act, the relevant time was therefore when the claimant first knew of the findings of the expert report, which was in September 1992. The Court of Appeal said: 8.003

"The claimant knew he was deaf. The claimant knew, once Mr Maqsood Ali had told him, that exposure to noise could cause deafness. Equally, he would know that the ageing process could cause deafness. But he did not and could not know whether his deafness had been caused by ageing or noise. Nor could Mr Maqsood Ali, nor his solicitor, nor any other layman. He could only find that out with the help of expert advice."

The Court of Appeal therefore held that the judge was wrong to hold that the mere fact of seeking that advice fixed him with knowledge for the purposes of s.14.

Comment: Therefore, for limitation purposes, where relevant knowledge can only be obtained through expert evidence, time will only start to run once that evidence is obtained.   8.004

Sniezek v. Bundy (Letchworth) Ltd [2000] **P.I.Q.R. P213**

This case before the Court of Appeal (Simon Brown and Judge L.JJ. and Bell J.) raised the issue of whether a personal injury claimant had knowledge for the purposes of s.14 Limitation Act 1980 (the "1980 Act"), and whether the judge was right to exercise his discretion under s.33 of the Act.   8.005
Section 14 of the 1980 Act, so far as it is material, provides:

"(1) . . . in section 11 . . . of this Act references to a person's date of knowledge are references to the date on which he first had knowledge of the following facts -

(a) that the injury in question was significant; and
(b) that the injury was attributable in whole or in part to the act or omission which is alleged to constitute negligence, nuisance or breach of duty; and
(c) the identity of the defendant;

. . . and knowledge that any acts or omissions did or did not, as a matter of law, involve negligence, nuisance or breach of duty is irrelevant."

The material provisions of s.33 of the 1980 Act are as follows:

"(1) If it appears to the court that it would be equitable to allow an action to proceed having regard to the degree to which —

(a) the provisions of s.11 . . . of this Act prejudice the plaintiff or any person whom he represents; and

(b) any decision of the court under this sub-section would prejudice the defendant or any person whom he represents;

the court may direct that those provisions shall not apply to the action, or shall not apply to any specified cause of action to which the action relates."

8.006   The claimant was a Hungarian national who started working for the defendant as a cleaner in 1972. In early 1984, after being moved to a new section, he became aware of a burning sensation on his lips and in his throat. In March 1989, when his symptoms had become severe, he was dismissed from his employment. In May 1990 his GP referred him to hospital but the investigations were clear.

In the same year he went to see his union solicitors who requested a report from a Dr R.M. Rudd, a consultant physician. In January 1991 the expert reported to the union's solicitors that there was no evidence to support the view that the claimant's symptoms were attributable to his work. However, in mid-1992 a hospital doctor wrote to the claimant's GP that, in his opinion, the burning sensation in the claimant's throat was most probably due to the chemicals and fumes that he had been exposed to for seven years in December 1992. The claimant then consulted the solicitors who would represent him at trial. They instructed a senior ENT Registrar, who examined the claimant in October 1993.

A key date was January 1994 when the ENT Registrar reported that it was difficult to prove that the claimant was actually experiencing the symptoms he claimed. However, he said that it seemed likely that he may well have suffered from some hyper-sensitisation of his upper aerodigestive tract which had left him with symptoms of a burning sensation.

After pre-action discovery in 1997, following examination of the mask used by the claimant when he was working, the ENT Registrar, by then a consultant otolaryngologist, concluded that there might be a basis for some of the claimant's symptoms having occurred as a result of exposure at his workplace, but that there was a large physiological overplay involved.

Nevertheless, in June 1998 counsel advised that the claimant had a reasonable case against the defendant and proceedings were issued on September 14, 1998.

The judge held that although the claimant had long believed that he had suffered injury, he only had knowledge for purposes of s.14 of the 1980 Act after the consultant's report in 1994. The defendant appealed.

8.007   The Court of Appeal referred to the cases of:

- *Nash v. Elli Lillie and Co.* [1993] 1 W.L.R. 782;

- *Spargo v. North Essex District Health Authority* [1997] P.I.Q.R. 235; and

- *O'Driscoll v. Dudley Health Authority* [1998] Lloyd's Rep. Med. 210.

These cases distinguished between:

- a claimant who had a firm belief that he had a significant injury attributable to his working conditions, whatever contrary advice he received; and

- a claimant who merely believed that he might or probably did have such an injury but was not sure and had to have expert advice.

The Court of Appeal held that the former was knowledge for the purposes of s.14 of the 1980 Act. The court further held that the claimant in this case fell into that category: he had possessed the relevant knowledge from 1989, when his symptoms were severe and he was dismissed from his employment. The Court of Appeal did not accept the submission that a claimant cannot know that he has an injury, or that it is significant just because medical experts advise that no injury can be found.

However, the court held that the judge was right to exercise his discretion under s.33 of the 1980 Act to disapply the provisions of ss11 and 14 because the claimant had made reasonable efforts to seek medical and other advice and to progress the claim. The allegation of prejudice to the defendant by reason of delay was not made out; nor was the allegation that the claim should not be allowed to proceed because it was weak.

The important point was that the claimant continued to believe that he had an injury which had been caused by conditions at work, despite repeated expert advice to the contrary.

Comment: This case is of relevance to experts acting in an advisory   **8.008**
capacity rather than in a reporting capacity to the court. Although all three of the judges in this case agreed that the application of s.14 of the 1980 Act turns on the facts of the case, experts should be aware that simply because they do not support a claimant's claim of injuries, this does not mean that time has not started running for the purposes of the 1980 Act. On the other hand, hard cases like the present case can always be catered for under s.33 of the 1980 Act.

CHAPTER 9
Single joint experts

9.001   The Lord Chancellor's Department report "Emerging Findings — An Early Evaluation of the Civil Justice Reforms", published in March 2001, highlights the single joint expert as one of seven "key new features" of the CPR. The impetus behind single joint experts is the desire to save time and costs in a manner which is proportionate to the issues in the case.

The idea of the single joint expert caused much concern before the implementation of the CPR. However, guidance is contained in the Vice-Chancellor's Working Party draft Code of Guidance on Expert Evidence. Guidance can also be found in the Practice Directions for the various tracks, the Commercial Court Guide, the Queen's Bench Guide and the Chancery Guide. For example, the guidelines for the conduct of fast-track cases indicate that single joint experts will be the rule rather than the exception (see paragraph 3.9(4) of the Practice Direction to Part 28), whereas the Commercial Court Guide provides that cases in the Commercial Court are frequently of a size and of a complexity such that the use of single joint experts is not appropriate (see paragraph H2.3).

Indeed, the varied use of the single joint expert is one of the most noticeable themes to emerge in the two years following the introduction of the CPR. The courts, and in particular, the Court of Appeal, have also conveyed the clear message that the CPR do not provide a presumption that a single joint expert will be instructed in every case. Various members of the judiciary have spoken and written on the varied use of the single joint expert. In his address to the first conference of the Expert Witness Institute, Lord Bingham said that there was everything to be said for a single joint expert when the expert issue is relatively uncontroversial and on the periphery of the case. However, he indicated that he found it more difficult to see how the procedure can work where the issue is highly controversial and central to the case. May L.J. at the October 2000 conference agreed that there will be cases where the balance of justice requires that a party should be entitled to instruct and call their own expert. Jacob J. expressed similar thoughts in KPMG's *The Forensic Accountant*, Issue 19, 1999: "There are obvious candidates. Take for instance, a dispute between a home-owner and a builder about some roofing work: the home-owner says the job was not done properly, the builder says it was — only a few thousand pounds are at stake. It makes sense to send in a local surveyor to look and form an opinion". However: "I do not believe that the single expert will be used in relation to major areas of contention in large cases".

9.002   Unsurprisingly, therefore, there have been several cases since the introduction of the CPR on the desire of parties to instruct experts in addition to the previously agreed single joint expert. The courts have shown themselves willing to accommodate parties in this respect. The clearest guidance to date on the question of whether a party should be permitted to adduce further expert evidence can be found in *Daniels v. Walker* and *Pattison v. Cosgrove* (see below). At the end of the day, it seems that if your case is complex enough, you will be allowed your own expert in addition to the single joint expert.

This is not to say that the courts have not embraced the concept of the single joint expert. Several of the cases reported below indicate the judges' satisfaction with the use of a single joint expert in the cases before them. Certainly, the Lord Chancellor's Department appears to believe that the system of the single joint expert is working well: the March 2001 report concludes: "The use of single joint experts appears to have worked well. It is likely that their use has contributed to a less adversarial culture, earlier settlement and may have cut costs".

S (a minor) v. Birmingham Health Authority (July 9, 1999) unreported

This case before Curtis J. examines the extent to which, under the CPR, it is   9.003
appropriate to limit the parties in a complex multi-track clinical negligence case to instructing a single joint expert.

The claimant was born on March 4, 1982. The cause of action turned on the alleged failure of the health authority's agents to perform a prompt and proper caesarean operation on the claimant's mother. The claimant suffered cerebral palsy, microcephaly and various other symptoms. It was acknowledged that the case was extremely complex. If there were to be damages, they would be large. In April 1999, both parties' solicitors, who were experienced in this sort of work, went before the district judge with an agreed order for multi-track case management directions. The appeal in question was the claimant's appeal against one of the orders made by the district judge, which was that the parties should jointly instruct a consultant neo-natal paediatrician to report on causation. The parties were then required also to consider whether any of the other experts could be jointly instructed. The claimant appealed, seeking to rely on his own experts.

Curtis J. held that the appointment of a joint expert was inappropriate in this case. He said that the judge's order that the parties should choose a particular expert, and should do so jointly, seemed to be premature:

> "In my view each side should be entitled to have its own expert to call and the order that a joint expert be instructed is inappropriate . . . I am not saying that a time may not come when the court will . . . have to suggest a court expert . . . but it is certainly not to be done at this stage."

Comment: The interest of this case lies in the judge's assessment that in   9.004
complex multi-track clinical negligence cases it is preferable for each party, initially at least, to have its own expert to ensure that a full case is presented in the pleadings. In the view of Curtis J., the decision of whether to instruct a joint expert could be considered later, in the light of the issues extracted by the experts.

It should be noted however that some believe that this first instance decision was wrongly decided in the context of clinical negligence cases, or at least, that it is wrong in view of the decision in *Daniels v. Walker* (see below). In the *Daniels v. Walker* case, the Court of Appeal said that the starting position (if not the finishing position) is that a single joint expert should be instructed, wherever possible.

Daniels v. Walker [2000] 1 W.L.R. 1382

9.005   In this case the issue before the Court of Appeal (Lord Woolf M.R. and Latham L.J.) was a point "of some significance" as to the approach which judges should adopt when a single joint expert who has been jointly instructed makes a report and one side is unhappy with that report.

The facts arose from an accident in which the claimant was involved as a child. The single issue before the Court of Appeal was the nature of the care which the claimant would require in the future. The Court of Appeal said that the parties in the case were to be commended on agreeing that there should be a jointly instructed expert, by a Wendy Daykin, an occupational therapist.

However, the Court of Appeal also made some comments on the manner in which the single joint expert was instructed. The claimant's solicitors had written an instruction letter to the expert with which the defendant's solicitors were unhappy. Although the matter could have been expressed in a more satisfactory way by the claimant, the Court of Appeal commented that the defendant's solicitors should have taken up the ready remedy available to them, that is to say, issuing separate instructions to her. The Court of Appeal also commented that where the parties have agreed to instruct an expert, it is obviously preferable that the form of instruction should be agreed if possible. Failing agreement, the Court of Appeal said that it is perfectly proper for either separate instructions to be given by one of the parties or for supplementary instructions to be given by one of the parties.

The issue in this case arose on receipt of the report from the joint expert. The defendant was concerned at the extent of the care regime recommended by the joint expert and sought to obtain a further care report from another expert.

The appellants advanced two separate arguments before the Court of Appeal. The first argument was based upon the CPR. The second argument was based upon the Human Rights Act 1998 and the European Convention on Human Rights (albeit that the 1998 Act was not in force at the relevant time).

9.006   As to the CPR argument, the court referred to the overriding objective of the CPR; CPR r.35.1 (which places a duty on the court to restrict expert evidence) and CPR r.35.6 (dealing with the ability of the parties to put questions to experts). The court also referred to CPR r.35.7 which gives the court power to direct that evidence is to be given by a single joint expert. Having considered the relevant rules, the Court of Appeal said that the fact that a party has agreed to instruct a joint expert does not prevent that party being allowed facilities to obtain a report from another expert, or, if appropriate, to rely on the evidence of another expert. The Court of Appeal added that in substantial cases such as this, the correct approach is to regard the instruction of an expert jointly by the parties as the first step in obtaining expert evidence on a particular issue. The court added that it is to be hoped that in the majority of cases it will not only be the first step but the last step. However, if having obtained a joint expert's report, a party, for reasons which are not fanciful, wishes to obtain further information before making a decision as to whether or not there is a particular part (or indeed the whole) of the expert's report which he or she may wish to challenge, then he or she should, subject to the discretion of the court, be permitted to obtain that evidence.

The Court of Appeal helpfully provided further guidance as to the circumstances when this may occur:

- in the majority of cases, the sensible approach will not be to ask the court straightaway to allow the dissatisfied party to call a second expert;

- in a case where there is a modest sum involved, a court may take a more rigorous approach since it may be argued that where a modest amount is involved it would be disproportionate to obtain a second report;

- the dissatisfied party should first consider whether their concerns could be satisfied by asking questions on the joint report; and

- if a party, or both parties, obtain their own expert reports, then the decision as to what evidence should be called at trial should not be taken until there has been a meeting between the experts involved.

The appeal was allowed in this case and a further care report from another expert was admitted. However, the Court of Appeal noted that this would not be the case *"where it is suggested that the claimant would be unduly distressed, or anything of that nature, by the additional examination"*. 9.007

As to the human rights arguments, the defendant argued that having regard to the provisions of Article 6 of the European Convention on Human Rights (right to a fair trial), a refusal of the defendant's wish to instruct a second expert would conflict with Article 6 because it amounted either to barring the whole claim of the defendant or barring an essential part of that claim.

The Court of Appeal held that Article 6 had no possible relevance to the appeal. The court said that, even if the Act had been in force, it would be highly undesirable if the consideration of case management issues was made more complex by the injection into them of Article 6-style arguments. The Court of Appeal said that it hoped that judges would be robust in resisting any attempt to introduce such arguments.

Comment: This was the first case in which the issue of instructing an expert, in addition to a single joint expert, was raised. The Court of Appeal conveyed the clear message that the fact that a party has agreed to instruct a joint expert does not prevent that party from obtaining a report from another expert, if appropriate. 9.008

Oxley v. Penwarden (July 21, 2000) unreported

In this case the Court of Appeal (Kennedy and Mantell L.JJ.) issued a reminder that the CPR do not provide a presumption that a single joint expert will be instructed in every case, particularly not in clinical negligence claims where causation of injury is at issue. 9.009

The claimant sued the defendant in negligence for failing to diagnose a vascular ischaemic condition in his leg, which led to the leg having to be amputated above the knee. The defendant denied negligence, and asserted that his diagnosis of the claimant's symptoms as a superficial thrombosis and/or a torn muscle was entirely reasonable.

The Court of Appeal noted that even from these few facts it is apparent that the central issues on liability centred around medical questions which could only be resolved by expert evidence. Nevertheless, at the case management conference, the judge directed, against the parties' wishes, that if the parties failed to agree on a single expert, the court would take it upon itself to appoint one. The Court of Appeal highlighted the notes to CPR r.35.7 which state:

> "There is no presumption in favour of the appointment of a single joint expert, except in cases allocated to the fast track. The object is to do away with the calling of multiple experts where, given the nature of the issue over which the parties are at odds, that is not justified".

The Court of Appeal held that this was a case where it was necessary for the parties "to have the opportunity of investigating causation through an expert of their own choice and, further, to have the opportunity of calling that evidence before the court". The court noted that it is inevitable in a case such as this that parties will find it difficult to agree on the appointment of a single expert. Further, it would not be right for the court to select a single expert from one particular school of thought since that would effectively decide an essential question in the case without the opportunity for challenge.

9.010   **Comment:** This is one in a number of helpful decisions by the Court of Appeal on CPR r.35.7. It is clear from these cases that the Court of Appeal will allow each side their own expert instead of a single joint expert if such a course is both proportionate and just.

Takenaka (UK) Limited v. Frankl, **The Independent, December 11, 2000**

9.011   In this case, Alliott J. unhesitatingly accepted the evidence of a single joint expert following analysis of the defendant's laptop computer and the e-mail traffic disclosed by it.

The case arose out of the claimants' action for damages for libel arising from the admitted publication of three admittedly defamatory e-mails sent to two officers of the first claimant. The e-mails were sent under the pseudonymous signature "Christina Realtor". The only issue at trial was whether the defendant was the real author and publisher of the e-mails. The claimants had spent months and considerable sums of money tracing the source of the e-mails to an account owned by a third party. That third party traced the use of that account to certain employees of the third party in Turkey, including the defendant. The defendant maintained that the allegations made against him were fabricated.

A single joint expert was therefore directed to give evidence by order of Deputy Master Fontain. That order named another expert, but, by consent, Mr Terence Bates was substituted. In accordance with CPR r.35.7, Mr Bates was instructed by both the claimant and the defendant. He prepared a preliminary report which analysed the contents of the computer which the defendant had used. The report concluded that since some of the traces of Hotmail activity matched closely with the dates and times of the malicious e-mails, it was "most probably" the computer used by the defendant that was the source of the Christina Realtor e-mails.

Interestingly, Alliott J. noted that it might have been expected that that conclusion would have brought an end to the litigation. However, this was not so.

Accordingly, Mr Bates prepared a further report of 104 pages. This report concluded as follows:

"I had no knowledge of the physical arrangements for the sharing of this lap top in Turkey. However, consideration of the various timings of activity surrounding the sending of the e-mails in question together with some indications taken from the text of certain e-mails leads me to conclude that the operator using the name "Frankl" and the operator using the name "Christina Realtor" and "C_Realtro" were the same person. I am aware that in this case the level of proof required should be on the balance of probabilities. I am confident that in this case that level of proof has been reached and exceeded by the evidence recovered from the lap top computer".

Alliott J. said that counsel for the defendant correctly reminded him that this is trial by judge alone and not trial by an expert. However, the judge remarked: "a judge tries the case upon the evidence, and in this case the expert evidence is of the highest quality in an arcane field in which the judge must be guided by that expert evidence". Further, the judge noted that Mr Bates embarked upon his investigation from an entirely neutral base, instructed both by the claimant and the defendant: "there could be no question of partisan bias, which is not unknown in the world of experts". The judge also remarked that both in his written reports and in his oral evidence the expert provided compelling evidence, which, despite the defendant's vehement denial, the judge unhesitatingly accepted. Alliot J. concluded that Mr Bates' evidence amounted to an overwhelming endorsement of the claimants' claims which he said the defendants should have recognised at a much earlier stage. Alliot J. found that the defendant was the author and publisher of the three e-mails.

Comment: This case provides an example of a good use of the single joint expert. It is also an example of an area in which the judge will be very happy to be guided by the expert, without allowing him to decide the matter for the court.   9.012

Pattison v. Cosgrove, The Times, February 13, 2001

Neuberger J. considered in this case whether the report of an expert instructed by one party should be admissible in addition to the report of a single joint expert.   9.013

The parties in a boundary dispute agreed in pursuance of CPR Part 35 that a report should be prepared by an expert instructed by them jointly. However, the defendant was unhappy with the report and applied for permission to instruct an expert of his own, who was already a witness of fact in the proceedings. The application was refused and he appealed.

Neuberger J. held that in determining whether to allow the evidence of second expert, in addition to the evidence of an expert instructed jointly under CPR Part 35, the factors to be considered were:

- the nature of the dispute;

- the number of issues on which the expert evidence was relevant;

- the reason for requiring the second expert;

- the amount at stake or the nature of the issues at stake;

- the effect of permitting a second expert report on the conduct of the trial;

- the delay that might be caused in the conduct of the proceedings;

- any other special features; and

- the overall justice to the parties.

In this case, the disputed matters were mostly factual and required expert evidence. The defendants had received a report calling into question the conclusions of the first expert, and the second expert had been involved in the case before litigation commenced and was to be called as witness of fact. The admission of the second report would have had little effect on the conduct of the case, and the likely hearing date was so far in the future that it would not be affected. If the second report were not allowed, the defendants would have an understandable sense of grievance, whilst if the report were allowed, it would not adversely affect the claimants as they too would have the opportunity to instruct their own expert if they so desired. Accordingly, having regard to all the circumstances, the admission of the second expert's evidence would be allowed.

9.014   **Comment:**   This case will be welcome to those who are concerned that instructing a single joint expert may take any control of the expert evidence out of their hands. In this case, following the lead of *Daniels v. Walker*, the court showed itself willing, even in a simple boundary dispute, to allow additional expert evidence if that was what justice required.

Carlson v. Townsend [2001] E.W.C.A. Civ. 511, New Law 201047002

9.015   This appeal before the Court of Appeal (Simon Brown, Brooke and Mance L.JJ.) raised an important point of practice about the disclosure of medical reports under the Pre-Action Protocol for Personal Injury Claims.

The claimant suffered a back injury whilst he was employed by the defendant as a care assistant. The injury was caused, in particular, through repeatedly having to lift and move the defendant's disabled adult son.

Pursuant to paragraphs 3.14 and 3.16 of the Pre-Action Protocol for Personal Injury Claims, the claimant gave the defendant a list of three names of consultant orthopaedic surgeons. The relevant provisions of the Pre-Action Protocol were as follows:

"3.14 Before any party instructs an expert he should give the other party a list of the name(s) of one or more experts in the relevant speciality whom he considers are suitable to instruct.

3.16 Within 14 days the other party may indicate an objection to one or more of the named experts. The first party should then instruct a mutually acceptable expert."

Other provisions also considered by the Court of Appeal included paragraphs 3.17 to 3.21.

The defendant objected to one of the three names proposed by the claimant. On that basis, the claimant instructed one of the remaining two, a Mr Trevett. Having obtained Mr Trevett's report, however, the claimant then declined to disclose it and instead instructed another expert, Dr Smith, who was not one of those originally named. The claimant was ordered to disclose Mr Trevett's report in July 2000. This order was overturned on appeal.

The Court of Appeal considered the following key questions: 9.016

- did the claimant's refusal to disclose Mr Trevett's report constitute a failure to comply with the Protocol?

- even assuming that it did, could the court properly then order the report's disclosure?

The basis of the defendant's request was that she interpreted the Pre-Action Protocol procedure as leading to the appointment of a joint expert. She therefore argued that, as Mr Trevett had been instructed on a joint basis, a copy of his report should be delivered to her at the same time as it was delivered to the claimant. The claimant's interpretation was that Mr Trevett had been instructed by the claimant only, not the defendant.

At first instance, Dickinson J. held that Mr Trevett was to be regarded as jointly instructed by both parties. On that approach, both parties had an equal right to see his report.

The Court of Appeal disagreed. It held that the Protocol provided for a prac-   9.017
tice whereby experts objectionable to one party were eliminated at the outset, and with them, an obvious barrier to the prospect of ultimately agreeing the expert evidence. This, however, did not amount to holding that by giving the other side the opportunity to object to a proposed expert, a party was waiving in advance the privilege which would otherwise attach to the report being obtained. The Court of Appeal referred specifically to CPR r.35.7 which relates to the instruction of a single joint expert. CPR r.35.7 provides that each party is entitled to give instructions to the expert. In those circumstances, there is plainly joint instruction of the expert resulting in both parties having equal liability for his fees and an equal right to see his report. However, this is not the practice provided for in the Protocol: "jointly selected the expert in a real sense has been; jointly instructed, however, he is not".

In addition, although the Protocol plainly encourages and promotes the voluntary disclosure of medical reports, it does not specifically require this. Withholding Mr Trevett's report did not constitute non-compliance with the Protocol, although the instruction of Dr Smith, without giving the defendant an opportunity to object, plainly did. Paragraphs 2.1 and 2.3 of the Practice Direction relating to protocols provides the court with various sanctions for non-compliance with a protocol. In the case at hand, the claimant had still to obtain the necessary permission from the court to call Dr Smith. The defendant would almost certainly, if she so wished, be permitted to call an expert of her choice. The court would, after all, know that one expert at least, Mr Trevett, had reported less favourably on the claimant's cause than Dr Smith. One sanction not available to the court, however, was to override the claimant's privilege in Mr Trevett's report. On that basis the appeal was dismissed.

9.018   **Comment:**   The Court of Appeal was of the view that the introduction of Pre-Action Protocols, and of the procedures they suggested for the obtaining of expert evidence, represented a major step forward in the administration of justice. Under the former regime before the CPR, nothing very effective seemed to happen until a writ was issued close to the end of the primary limitation period. Insofar as the use of experts was concerned, there were often complaints that they appeared to be antagonistic towards the party who was not paying for their services. Thus, it was unlikely that the report would be accepted. This led to further delay and expense while the other side instructed their own expert, who might well adopt an equally antagonistic position.

> The Court of Appeal quoted Lord Woolf's Final Report on Access to Justice in this context:
>
> "Protocols will also be an important means of promoting economy in the use of expert evidence, and particularly encouraging the parties to use a single expert wherever possible. Unless this happens before the commencement of proceedings, it will frequently be too late because the parties will already have established an entrenched relationship with their own expert."

The Court of Appeal interpreted the intention behind paragraphs 3.14 and 3.16 of the Protocol on Personal Injury Claims to be that defendants could identify at an early stage if the claimant was intending to use an expert whom they regarded as partisan and whose report they were unlikely to accept. The Court of Appeal's view was that the protocols were guides to good litigation and pre-litigation practice. Importantly, it held that the purpose of paragraphs 3.14 to 3.21 did not amount to the instruction of an expert on a joint basis.

Knight v. Sage Group plc (April 28, 1999) unreported

9.019   This case is considered in the section below entitled "Content, form and purpose of expert reports"; however, it also raises interesting issues relating to the use of single joint experts.

North Holdings Ltd v. Southern Tropics Ltd [1999] 2 B.C.L.C. 625

9.020   This case is considered in the section below entitled "Weighing up the evidence (valuation)"; however, it also raises interesting issues relating to the use of single joint experts.

Field v. Leeds City Council (2000) 17 E.G. 165

9.021   This case is considered in the section above entitled "Considerations when identifying who should act as expert"; however, it also raises interesting issues relating to the instruction of single joint experts.

Kranidiotes v. Paschali [2001] E.W.C.A. Civ. 357, New Law 201036201

9.022   This case is considered in the section below entitled "Weighing up the evidence (company)"; however, it also raises interesting issues relating to the use of single joint experts.

CHAPTER 10
Timing and delay

There is no rule in the CPR which explicitly deals with the importance of serv‑ **10.001**
ing expert evidence in good time. However, there have been several cases which
emphasise the importance of prompt service. One reason for this is that expert
reports now have a purpose over and above providing evidence at trial. They
serve as a means of exchanging helpful information before trial, in the hope that
a settlement will be reached, thus saving time and expense. Accordingly, the
courts have taken a dim view of parties who hold back expert evidence until
close to trial. Behaviour of this kind will, at best, attract cost penalties, and, at
worst, prompt the court to make an order that the party cannot rely upon that
evidence.

Expert shopping is another cause of delay. This occurs where parties continue
instructing experts until they find one whose evidence favours their case. Whilst
the courts have acknowledged a party's right to seek further expert opinions,
they appear to have taken a firm stance against this causing any delay to the
proceedings.

Baron v. Lovell [2000] P.I.Q.R. P20

In this case, the Court of Appeal (Lord Woolf M.R., Brooke and Robert **10.002**
Walker L.JJ.) emphasised the importance of disclosing an expert report
promptly.

The claimant was a groundsman. In September 1995 the tractor he was driv‑
ing was hit by the defendant's car. The defendant was subsequently convicted of
driving without due care and attention. The claimant commenced proceedings
against the defendant, seeking damages for personal injury sustained in the col‑
lision. The defendant admitted his liability to compensate the claimant, but put
the claimant to strict proof as to the quantum of damages.

The appeal related to the substantially delayed service of medical expert evi‑
dence by the defendant.

The claimant was seen by the claimant's medical expert, Mr Marchon, in
May 1996. Mr Marchon saw the claimant again sixteen months later, in
September 1997, for the purposes of a second report. Mr Wetherill was
instructed as an expert by the defendant's solicitors on August 22, 1998 to
examine the claimant in connection with the proceedings. He examined the
claimant on January 6, 1999. He sent his report to the defendant's solicitors on
February 18, 1999, but they did not disclose it to the claimant's solicitors until
June 16, 1999 (at the pre-trial hearing).

Automatic directions applied in this case. The defendant was accordingly **10.003**
obliged to disclose any expert medical evidence on which he sought to rely
within 10 weeks (*i.e.* by November 20, 1998). If the defendant failed to do so, he
would not be permitted to call any such evidence at the trial, except with the
leave of the court or with the agreement of the claimant. The defendant's solic‑
itors did not mention the ten-week deadline to Mr Wetherill when they

instructed him. When challenged as to why they had not disclosed Mr Wetherill's report to the claimant earlier, the defendant's solicitors said that they had intended to disclose it at the same time as they made a payment into court on April 26, 1999 and that they thought they had served it then. They apologised for the oversight. The judge hearing the original application had decided that the defendant would not be permitted to call his medical expert (nor submit any written expert evidence) at the trial of the action, which was fixed for August 1999.

The defendant challenged that decision. However, the Court of Appeal agreed with the judge. Brooke L.J. was not impressed by the defendant's argument:

> "if ever there was a case which ought to have settled at the pre-trial review, if the expert's report and updated witness statements had been served in good time before the review, it was this one. If it had, there would have been a saving of six sets of professional fees for a full day's hearing at the trial".

The defendant's solicitors raised a number of points in their defence.

- They complained that there had been no earlier order made in respect of expert evidence, much less an "unless" order. Brooke L.J. was of the view that, by an automatic direction, they were obliged to serve the report within 10 weeks of the trigger date and, in the absence of agreement or a court order, they were thereafter at the mercy of the court, which could refuse leave to adduce expert evidence if it considered it unjust to admit it at a late stage.

- They complained that there would be no delay in the trial taking place should the defendant be given permission to rely on Mr Wetherill's evidence. Brooke L.J. stated that this complaint;

  > "reveals a fundamental misconception . . . pre-trial disclosure obliges the parties to disclose to each other the substance of the evidence on which they intend to rely at the trial . . . it is not legitimate to serve out of date statements and then hope to be allowed to update them in a radical way just before the trial . . . Consultant orthopaedic surgeons are busy people and it is quite wrong for trials to be delayed, and for the possibility of making an effective Part 36 offer to be rendered nugatory because of a late service of an expert statement, followed by an even later "updated" meeting between experts."

- Brooke L.J. was also unsympathetic to the defendant's solicitors' view that "there was no way the defendant could keep to this timetable". This lack of sympathy may have been linked to the fact that they had not informed Mr Wetherill of the timetable for automatic directions. Further, the defendant's solicitors complained that the claimant's solicitors had not pursued the question of Mr Wetherill's report after March 3, 1999 or sought a debarring order. Brooke L.J. considered that the claimant's solicitors were not obliged to do so. As the defendant's solicitors were requiring the permission of the court in order to adduce the expert report, it was in the defendant's interest that such permission should be sought promptly. The Court of Appeal found that it was definitely not "in the spirit of Woolf to delay disclosing it deliberately, as she [one of the defendant's solicitors] intended, until the day a Part 36 payment was made".

Comment: This case shows that the courts have, since the introduction of the CPR, become more stringent in their enforcement of automatic directions in personal injury cases. Strong grounds will be necessary to convince a court to allow any expert evidence once the time limit for exchange of reports has expired under the automatic directions. In coming to a decision, the courts will take into account differences between the reports and reasons and motives for the delay. The courts will not be impressed if the report has been delayed for tactical reasons. It is, in any event, strongly recommended that experts inform themselves as to the date by which a final report needs to be served in particular proceedings, to avoid the situation which arose in this case.

10.004

Jenkins v. Grocott (July 30, 1999) **unreported**

This case before Hale J. related to the late service of expert evidence.

10.005

This was a claim for damages arising out of a road traffic accident. The claimant suffered a serious head injury whilst riding as a pillion passenger on a motorcycle driven by one of his friends. Judgment was entered in his favour but the quantum of damages remained in dispute. The main issue centred around past and future care.

A preliminary issue arose as to whether the defendant should be able to adduce the evidence of a care expert. Her report was dated December 1998 and updated in April 1999, but was not disclosed to the claimant's advisors until June 1999, only four weeks before the trial and far too late for the claimant to be able to commission his own report. The claimant relied on the evidence of four experts, namely three medical experts and an employment consultant. However, they had not thought it necessary to commission a separate care report on the ground that they believed the defendant would not be adducing that type of evidence. Had they known that the defendant was proposing to rely on her evidence, they would have considered getting their own report and probably would not have taken the risk of proceeding without one.

Hale J. considered that this was "a classic illustration of a situation which the new civil procedural rules are designed to prevent. They provide for an early isolation of the issues on which expertise is required and identification of the expert who will be asked to advise the court". Hale J. went on to add that, wherever possible, a single, jointly instructed expert was to be preferred.

However, the overriding objective of the CPR was to enable the court to "deal with cases justly". The judge's view was that this included ensuring that the parties were on an equal footing. Hale J. considered that the parties were scarcely on an equal footing if one of them was able effectively to spring on the other expert evidence which could not have reasonably been foreseen and which there was now no realistic opportunity of countering. It was accepted that the defendant was not deliberately taking a tactical advantage and that the late disclosure was a mistake. However, it put the claimant at some disadvantage.

On the facts of the case, Hale J. considered that it was relevant and not prejudicial to the claimant's case that Ms Booth could give evidence of the costs of particular options. In addition, the evidence which Ms Booth could give was unlikely to weigh heavily against the more expert views available on each side. On that basis, the defendant was allowed to adduce his expert report.

10.006   **Comment:**   It is clear that the expectation from the court is that this type of situation should not occur under the CPR. As Hale J. commented, it remained to be seen "how far the new procedures, not only in the rules but also in the pre-action protocol for personal injury claims, will inhibit the practice of instructing several experts and choosing the one whose views happen to suit those of the instructing party".

Purdy v. Cambran (December 17, 1999) New Law 2991222106

10.007   This case before the Court of Appeal (Swinton–Thomas and May L.JJ. and Singer J.) was mainly concerned with inordinate delay of service of expert reports and the prejudicial effect of the delay on the defendant. The interest of the case lies in the fact that the inordinate delay was a result of "expert shopping".

The claimant brought a claim in respect of serious injuries sustained by him in a road traffic accident. He issued proceedings about a week before the expiry of the limitation period of his claim. The action then proceeded exceedingly slowly. Eventually, the defendant applied to strike out the action for want of prosecution and as an abuse of process. The claimant's justification for the delay was by reference to difficulties that arose in relation to one of the experts instructed on his behalf. The judge did not accept that justification and struck the action out. The claimant appealed.

The Court of Appeal first made a general comment about the speed at which this case had been pursued:

> "It is to be hoped that, with case management by judges, delays such as have occurred in this case will never occur again. It is now over 10 years since this accident occurred and the case has not been tried. That is undoubtedly a scandalous state of affairs."

The court then considered the issue of the expert reports.

The first report for the claimant dated October 1990 was from Mr Rajaratnam, a registrar at the Princess Margaret hospital. He set out the injuries that the claimant sustained in the accident and described them as multiple fractures. The second report was from Mr Quinnell, an orthopaedic consultant surgeon. In August 1991, there was a further consultant orthopaedic surgeon report by Mr Norris. Mr Jefferson, a neurologist, advised in May 1992. There was a further report from Mr Quinnell in May 1992. The defendant instructed Mr Berkin, a consultant orthopaedic surgeon. His first report was dated February 1993. Mr Quinnell reported again on behalf of the appellant in February 1994 and stated that he agreed with the defendant's expert that the effects of the accident added to the pre-existing arthritic change. As a result of what Mr Quinnell said in that report, the claimant and his advisors decided to obtain the opinion of an alternative orthopaedic expert. It was not until February 1995 that a report was obtained from the next consultant, Mr Compton. On this, the claimant's counsel said that the judge at trial was wrong when he referred to the claimant's "expert shopping": "the decision to obtain a different expert was not something which was done on a whim, but . . . the claimant was plainly entitled to obtain an opinion from a different expert". The Court of Appeal found that there was substance in that submission. However, if further evidence was to be obtained, then it was vital to have obtained the alternative evidence speedily.

A further complication arose in relation to the expert evidence when the defendant's expert died in August 1998. The claimant's counsel submitted that this did not cause the defendant substantial prejudice since it was open to him to find a new expert. The Court of Appeal found that this was not a realistic approach. The defendant could have consulted another orthopaedic surgeon. However, that surgeon would not have had the advantage of having examined the claimant over a period of time. The defendant was also perfectly entitled to say that Mr Berkin was their chosen expert: "he had expressed an opinion which was favourable to their case and they are now deprived of the great advantage of having him as a witness to go into the witness box and give the evidence that is contained in his report". There was no doubt in the court's mind that the defendant had suffered substantial prejudice by reason of the death of his expert witness which occurred a long time after the case should have been heard. On that basis, the Court of Appeal upheld the judge's decision to strike out the claim. **10.008**

In this context, May L.J. reminded the parties of the purpose of the CPR. The court should ensure, so far as practical, that cases are dealt with expeditiously and fairly because "delay is, and always has been, the enemy of justice".

Comment: In terms of the "expert shopping" point, the Court of Appeal recognised the claimant's right to obtain a further report if he considered it nec- essary. This, however, should have been done expeditiously and should not have delayed the action any further. **10.009**

Calenti v. North Middlesex NHS Trust (March 2, 2001) New Law 201047002

The interest of this case lies in the defendant's attempt, two weeks before trial, to be granted permission to call the most suitably qualified medical expert in the area of relevant expertise. **10.010**

The claimant had brought an action for clinical negligence resulting from a viral illness she had suffered. The trial of the matter was listed for March 19, 2001 and liability was an issue. On February 16, 2001 the defendant made a late application for permission to rely on the medical report of a Dr Whitley. Dr Whitley appeared to be an expert, if not the main expert, on the viral illness with which the case was concerned. It seemed that most of the relevant experts acknowledged Dr Whitley's writings, and drew on data that he seemed either to have produced or to have collated. The basis of the defendant's application was that, in the circumstances, justice would best be served by Dr Whitley being called.

Buckley J. considered that, whilst Dr Whitley's expertise could well have assisted the court in ascertaining the true situation as far as it was able to do so, the defendant had left the matter very late in the day. If any expert was to be brought in at this stage, it was extremely likely that questions would need to be put to him and that arrangements would need to be made for him to meet with the other experts involved in the case. Given the shortness of time remaining before the trial, Buckley J. was of the view that it was doubtful whether that could be done.

Further, the defendant had known of Dr Whitley's existence for at least four years and there was no real explanation, let alone excuse, for not seeking permission from the court earlier. Buckley J. also took into consideration the fact that the defendant had its own experts in this field and that they had been in touch with Dr Whitley. Therefore, insofar as they needed answers, explanations or information from him, they should have been able to get these. Buckley J. therefore concluded that "the only aspect that will be missing is Dr Whitley's own first hand view of the situation, but as I say, I think it is an inappropriate way of proceeding to leave it as late in the day as this". On that basis, the application was dismissed.

10.011   **Comment:** This is another reminder to think carefully and early about which experts should give evidence as the court will be unsympathetic to late applications.

CHAPTER 11

Weighing up the evidence

This section considers how expert evidence has been used by the courts since the **11.001** introduction of the CPR. It focuses, in particular, on how the courts balance competing evidence, when the courts are entitled to reject expert evidence and what type of expert evidence the courts find useful. The following general principles arise from the cases:

- rejecting expert evidence — a judge must always give detailed reasons why he has decided not to follow the expert evidence placed before him. It is especially important for a judge to provide clear reasons in circumstances where he rejects consistent evidence from more than one expert witness. Failure to meet these requirements will be a ground of appeal;

- competing expert evidence — the judge should not simply decide which opinion to accept. Instead, the court must decide the issue for itself, giving reasons why the evidence of one expert is preferred over that of another; and

- competing expert and factual evidence — the court should only prefer factual evidence on a specialised issue if the expert evidence is logically unsupportable.

For ease of reference, different subjects are covered in separate sections.

COMPANY

Secretary of State for Trade and Industry v. Baker (No. 5) [2000] 1 B.C.L.C. 523

The interest of this case lies in comments by the Court of Appeal (Morritt, **11.002** Walker and Mummery L.JJ.) on expert evidence used in proceedings against Mr Ronald Baker, a director of one of the Barings' subsidiaries.

In February 1995 the Barings banking group collapsed as a result of the unauthorised activities of Mr Nick Leeson, the General Manager of a Singapore subsidiary ("BFS"), who had made trading losses of some £827 million. The circumstances of the collapse were investigated by the Ministry of Finance in Singapore. In addition, the Secretary of State took director disqualification proceedings against ten respondents who were directors of Barings companies. The case against three directors went to trial and Parker J. found that they were unfit to hold office and should be disqualified. Mr Baker, as a director of the main merchant banking subsidiary, was disqualified for six years. Mr Baker appealed against the finding of unfitness and the disqualification order.

The main question which the Court of Appeal considered was whether

Mr Baker was unfit and should be disqualified. The points which arose in relation to expert evidence in this context are set out below.

11.003   The first point related to the independence of one of the expert witnesses, Mr Taylor, who gave evidence on behalf of the Secretary of State. In his evidence, he summarised the relevant facts. There was a suggestion that Mr Taylor, in view of his experience and qualification, could not only summarise the relevant facts but also "identify the failing on the part of the respondent". Mr Baker's counsel opposed that suggestion on the basis that Mr Taylor was not qualified to give expert evidence because he was not independent. This submission was upheld by the judge:

> "Insofar as he [Mr Taylor] has made use of his experience and expertise in explaining the background to the allegations which have been made, he has, of course, given the greatest assistance to the court. But, in my judgment, that is as far as he may go, given that he has de facto assumed the role of the office-holder in putting forward the Secretary of State's case".

The second point concerned the lack of expert evidence. At first instance, Mr Baker had argued that the failure of the Secretary of State to call expert evidence was fatal to the charge of unfitness made against him because "the court is left in the position of attempting to reach a decision on the appropriate and reasonable practice of a manager of a derivatives business within a complex global investment bank without any relevant evidence from a member of that profession". The judge rejected that submission. The Court of Appeal agreed. The issue was not whether Mr Baker was an incompetent operator in the financial products or derivatives market:

> "It is wrong to equate disqualification proceedings with a professional negligence claim. The standard of competence to be shown by a person as a director is a different question and is one of law."

11.004   The Court of Appeal's view was that the question as to whether Mr Baker had failed to achieve that standard was one for the court, and furthermore that very rarely would the evidence of an expert be admissible. This particular case was not one of those exceptions.

In addition, the Court of Appeal decided that it was a matter for the judge whether or not to accept the evidence of Mr Baker on matters pertaining to the derivatives market. There was no indication that the judge failed to understand any matter relevant to the decisions he had to make.

Finally, the Court of Appeal observed that "if Mr Baker had considered that expert evidence would be required at the trial then it was up to him to adduce it".

11.005   **Comment:** This case shows how the court will approach director disqualification proceedings in terms of expert evidence. Essentially, it would appear that the court will view the question of competence as a question of law which does not usually require expert evidence.

Kranidiotes v. Paschali [2001] E.W.C.A. Civ. 357, New Law 201036201

This case before the Court of Appeal (Aldous and Laws L.JJ.) related to an **11.006**
order terminating the appointment of a court-appointed joint expert engaged
to value the shares of a minority shareholder after a s.459 petition had been
presented.

The relevant company was Ecocolor Ltd (the "company"). The petitioner,
Mr Kranidiotes, was appointed a director of the company in June 1994. He was
also a minority shareholder. In the s.459 petition, he alleged that a series of
transactions, goods, services and cash to a value in excess of £100,000 had been
transferred out of the company and its wholly-owned subsidiary, Colorpave
Ltd, for the benefit of another company owned and controlled by Mr Paul
Paschali, who was the majority shareholder of the company.

There was a directions hearing. The order that was made at the hearing
required Mr Paschali to purchase the petitioner's entire shareholding in the
company "at a price equal to the appropriate market value as of April 5, 1998".
The relevant parts of the order he made are set out below:

> "2.0 a joint expert (the "joint expert") shall be appointed to prepare a   **11.007**
> report (the "report") as to the market value, in each case as at August 5,
> 1998 of:
>
> > 2.1 the entire issued share capital of Ecocolor Ltd;
> > 2.2 a shareholding comprising 20 shares in Ecocolor Ltd; and
> > 2.3 a shareholding comprising 33 shares in Ecocolor Ltd.
>
> 3.0 the identity of the joint expert shall be agreed between the petitioner
> and the respondents by May 19, 2000. Failing such agreement, either the
> petitioner or the respondents may apply to the district judge for his deter-
> mination of the identity of the joint expert. On the hearing of any such
> application the petitioner and the respondents shall each provide a list of
> their suggested candidates for the position of joint expert, such lists to
> number no more than 3 candidates each.
>
> 4.0 the joint expert shall be instructed in the following terms, namely:
>
> > 'you are jointly instructed by, on the one hand, the petitioner and,
> > on the other, the first and second respondents (together "the respon-
> > dents"). You are instructed to provide a report giving your opinion
> > as to the market value as between a willing purchaser and a will-
> > ing seller of certain shares in Ecocolor Ltd as at 5th August, 1998;
> > you shall provide your opinion of the market value as between a
> > willing purchaser and a willing seller, in each case as at 5th August,
> > 1998 of:
> > . . . [the particular shares]
> > the method and basis of valuation to be adopted shall be entirely in
> > your sole discretion taking into account normal accounting principles.
> > In the manner referred to below, the petitioner and the first respondent
> > shall be free to make such submissions in writing to you as each sees
> > fit on the method and basis which it is considered appropriate to

adopt. You shall give such weight if any as you think fit to any exist-ing accounts but you are not bound to accept any such accounts whether audited or not.

. . .

You shall serve on each of the petitioner and the respondents and file at court your report by 31st August, 2000. In preparing your report you shall undertake only such investigations and enquiries as are consistent with an overall fee of £10,000 . . . (or such higher figure as may be agreed between the parties . . .) for the production of the report . . .

6.0 there be liberty to each party and to the expert referred to above to apply to the court for any clarification or further directions needed'."

11.008   The judge chose the amount of £10,000 as the fee because the value of the shareholding claimed by the petitioner was thought by him not to exceed £130,000, but was thought by the respondent to have a value of about £14,000 to £15,000. The judge's aim was, therefore, to adopt a proportionate attitude to the trial.

The parties decided to instruct Mr Uglow of Deloitte & Touche as joint expert. He was given instructions by letter in similar terms to those set out in the order. Each side provided Mr Uglow with extensive written submissions. Having read these submissions, Mr Uglow realised that he could not deal with the matters raised in the submissions without exceeding the £10,000 limit. He therefore wrote to the court to raise this. He estimated that in order to carry out the investigations required he would need to do a complete re-audit of the accounts of the company and Colorpave for at least the previous three to four years. He had already spent £4,500 in fees and quoted a fee of £75,000 to carry out these full audits, with an estimate of £30,000 for producing figures based on a trial sampling.

Mr Uglow also raised with the court his approach to the valuation. His diffi-culty was in the requirement that he was to provide an opinion of the market shares as between a willing buyer and a willing seller. In his view, in an actual transaction, if the buyer became aware of allegations regarding the accounts, the most likely outcome would be that he would walk away from the transac-tion. At the very least, the buyer would require specific warranties and probably an earn-out mechanism. The approach which Mr Uglow decided to adopt was:

"to assume a somewhat artificial situation in which a buyer would be aware of the nature of the allegations . . . but would not be in a position to inves-tigate the allegations further. As a result he would base his view of value on that knowledge, the statutory accounts and detailed profit and loss accounts of the company, any budgets and forecasts available, and any relevant information in the public domain, for example, accounts of competitors."

As a result, he would expect to discount the value he placed on the company accordingly.

11.009   The judge concluded that the approach suggested by Mr Uglow was not consistent with the spirit of the order that he had made, and that the best course was to dispense with the services of Mr Uglow and to use a cheaper expert. The judge decided to choose Solomon Hare on the basis of an estimate of £20,000–£25,000 for similar work.

On appeal, it was argued that the judge had concentrated unnecessarily on questions of proportionality and costs and failed to consider whether the parties had made a binding agreement and whether the method to be adopted by Mr Uglow complied with the terms of the agreement.

The Court of Appeal upheld the judge's decision on the basis that he was right to base his judgment on the fact that he "expected a proportionate investigation of the facts to help him to produce a reasoned judgment, which of course would take into account the submissions of the parties". In terms of case management, the judge had three options: to go ahead with the approach of Mr Uglow; to give directions to Mr Uglow for another approach; or to obtain a report from an expert who would charge less to make a more detailed inquiry. The judge was entitled to choose the last of these. The Court of Appeal was satisfied that the judge was required to, and did, bear in mind the need for a proportionate approach. The judge had before him a cheaper route which he believed would enable a reasonable inquiry into the facts. On that basis the appeal was dismissed.

Comment: This case highlights the importance of proportionality in terms of the instruction of experts and the difficulty in balancing that with fairness. In addition, this is an example of the approach to be taken by a joint expert when that expert is in doubt over how to proceed.   **11.010**

EMPLOYMENT

Wood v. William Ball Ltd [1999] I.R.L.R. 773

This case before the Employment Appeal Tribunal (Morison J. Mr Dawson OBE and Mr Shrigley) was concerned with the proper procedure for obtaining expert evidence under s.2A(1) Equal Pay Act 1970 in the context of equal value work claims.   **11.011**

The nine appellants, who were all women, had made a complaint against their employers, William Ball Ltd, that they had been paid less than they were entitled to. The appellants were employed as cleaners/packers in William Ball's business, which manufactured and distributed kitchen, bedroom and office furniture. In broad terms, they were comparing the value of their work to that of the work done by a group of men called pickers/packers.

The applicants made an application to an employment tribunal to adjourn the case for preparation of an expert report pursuant to s.2(A)(i) Equal Pay Act 1970. In considering the request, the tribunal concluded that there were no reasonable grounds for determining that their work was of equal value to that of their comparitors. Consequently, the application to adjourn was refused and the originating application dismissed on the basis that they had no reasonable prospect of success. The tribunal's unanimous decision was that "there are no reasonable grounds for determining that the work of the applicants is of equal value to that of their comparitors. Consequently, these originating applications are not adjourned for the preparation of an expert's report but are dismissed as they have no reasonable prospect of success in respect of all the complaints".

The Employment Appeal Tribunal considered the procedure contemplated by s.2(A)(i) closely.

The particular wording of s.2(A)(i) was as follows:

> "Where on a complaint or reference made to an industrial tribunal under section 2 above a dispute arises as to whether any work is of equal value as mentioned in section 1(2)(c) above the tribunal may either:
>
> (a) proceed to determine that question; or
>
> (b) unless it is satisfied that there are no reasonable grounds for determining that the work is of equal value as so mentioned, require a member of the panel of independent experts to prepare a report with respect to that question; and
>
> (c) if it requires the preparation of a report under para (b) of this sub-section, it shall not determine that question unless it has received the report."

That statutory provision, which was the operative provision in this case, replaced an earlier provision which read as follows:

> "2(a)(I) where on a complaint or reference made to an industrial tribunal under section 2 above a dispute arises as to whether any work is of equal value as mentioned in section 1(ii)(c) above the tribunal shall not determine that question unless it is satisfied that there are no reasonable grounds for determining that the work is of equal value as so mentioned; or
>
> (b) it has required a member of the panel of independent experts to prepare a report with respect to that question and has received that report."

The Appeal Tribunal held that the fact that the original tribunal had concluded that there was no reasonable prospect of the applicants showing that their work was of equal value did not put an end to the case, but permitted the parties themselves to adduce expert evidence in support of their claim (which they could adduce at a further hearing).

The Appeal tribunal considered that Parliament's intention was that there be a two stage process. The first stage was to decide whether an expert report was to be obtained and if so by whom (*i.e.* by the tribunal or by the parties themselves). The second stage was to determine the matter on the basis of the expert evidence adduced, be it requested by the parties or by the tribunal. Therefore, where the tribunal refused to arrange an expert at the government's expense, the parties themselves should be free to do so by appointing their own expert.

11.012   It was unlikely that the parties would themselves have gone to the expense of investing in experts' reports before making an application to the tribunal that it should obtain a report itself. Therefore, it must have been Parliament's intention that the mere fact that an applicant failed to persuade a tribunal to order an independent report would not mean that a tribunal might not, in due course, reach a completely different conclusion based on expert evidence which the parties then produced. In coming to this conclusion, the Appeal Tribunal considered the whole regime (including the Employment Tribunal's (Constitution and Rules of Procedure) Regulations 1993 and explanatory notes to the new statutory procedure).

The Appeal Tribunal found that there had been a procedural mishap in that the original tribunal had moved from stage one (which was to ask whether they should commission a report) straight to stage two (to determine the matter themselves) without giving the parties an opportunity to adduce their own expert evidence.

The Appeal Tribunal looked at what the original tribunal actually thought it was deciding. It was clear from the way the tribunal had phrased its remit that it had set out to ask itself whether it should appoint an independent expert. However, it went on to decide more than that without giving the parties a proper opportunity of addressing the court on these issues. The original tribunal seemed to have failed to identify for itself and for the parties the precise issues that were before it. If the original tribunal's intention had been to judge the whole matter and not simply the question of whether an independent expert was required, then the tribunal should have notified the parties in advance that it was considering doing so. The parties should have been told that in the event that they failed to persuade the Tribunal to arrange for the appointment of an independent expert, their rights would be fully determined by the Employment Tribunal.

Comment: It seems that there are three ways to approach the procedure in s.2(A)(1). Under this section, the tribunal can: 11.013

- find that there are no reasonable grounds for determining that the applicant's work is of equal value, in which case the application must be dismissed;

- instruct an expert to report within a specified time and give directions for full hearing; or

- find that there are no reasonable grounds for determining the applicant's work as being of equal value on the basis of the evidence presented, but that the applicants should be given the opportunity of adducing expert evidence.

The Appeal Tribunal considered that the third way was the normal procedure where an application is made for the appointment of an expert by the tribunal, because one would not have anticipated by that stage that the parties themselves would have gone to the expense of engaging experts. What seems important here, is the expectation of the parties as to what the tribunal is actually determining at that particular hearing and any agreement made between the parties and/or the tribunal in this respect.

There were also references to Schedule 2 of the Industrial Tribunal (Constitution and Rules of Procedure) Regulations 1993 (particularly paragraphs 8 and 9), which provide some interesting guidance as to expert evidence procedure in the context of these types of proceedings.

Bank of Credit and Commerce International S.A. v. Ali (No. 3) [1999] 4 All E.R. 83

11.014   This case before Lightman J. was concerned with employment "stigma" cases following the collapse of the Bank of Credit and Commerce International ("BCCI").

BCCI collapsed in 1991 and went into compulsory liquidation in 1992. It had been insolvent since at least 1986 and the senior management had for many years been engaged in fraudulent activities designed to conceal the bank's financial position. At the same time, ordinary banking business was being carried on by ordinary employees who were unaware of the fraudulent activities. A number of employees were made redundant before the liquidation and most of the others were made redundant by the liquidators once it became clear that the bank would not continue as a going concern.

Many former employees brought proceedings against the bank, including "stigma claims" in which employees sought damages on the basis that the stigma of having worked for the bank was a hindrance to their subsequently obtaining further gainful employment. They claimed damages for (i) stigma; (ii) the financial loss occasioned to them by such stigma; and (iii) the loss the stigma in fact inflicted on them. One of the main hurdles facing the employees was to establish that they had suffered loss. In this context, the parties adduced expert evidence from a Mr Langman as to the state of the labour market since the date of the collapse of the bank; the hiring practices of employers and recruitment agencies; and the extent to which the applicants' previous employment with BCCI would influence their decision-making.

Lightman J. considered that there were matters which figured largely in Mr Langman's first report that were of no significance.

11.015   Firstly, Lightman J. considered that he could not attach any significant weight to Mr Langman's views as to the employees' employment prospects over the relevant period and the impact of stigma upon them. This was because, in evaluating the employment prospects, employment history, motivation and character of the employees, Mr Langman relied on interviews in which he accepted at face value and unquestioningly what they had said. As a result, it was quite clear to Lightman J. that Mr Langman only obtained a partial and superficial picture.

Secondly, the expert considered long-term unemployment figures and analyses of recruitment practices and the impact of stigma. Lightman J. considered that statistics provided no assistance in determining the significance of stigma in the case of the particular employees. It was therefore necessary to "look at each individual case separately and the particular job search technique".

In contrast, Lightman J. found particularly helpful the evidence given by Coutts, a company employed by BCCI to help its employees find new employment. This evidence showed that the prospects of obtaining fresh employment very much depended on the attitude of the individual client. Past employment by the bank, though a cause of anxiety on the part of clients and a possible ground for a prospective employer preferring another candidate with equal skills, did not deter prospective employers approaching Coutts to fill their vacancies. It was not seen by Coutts to be a substantial problem.

The judge also found helpful, in this context, evidence given by prospective employers and recruitment agencies. Lightman J. concluded from this that, "whilst stigma is capable of attaching to a former employee of the bank in the eyes of particular prospective employers and handicapping that former employee vis-à-vis that prospective employer, that can only be tested on a case-by-case examination of each prospective employer". There could, however, "be no presumption that it has come into play or will come into play on any particular application".

In seeking an explanation for the failure of the employees to obtain jobs, Lightman J. concluded from the expert evidence that it was necessary to have in mind the various considerations which may have operated on the minds of the prospective employers whom they approached. The judgment went on to consider those particular aspects.

Comment: The interest of this case lies in the particular subject matter at hand and a detailed analysis of evidence in "stigma" cases. It also provides confirmation that privileged material will lose its privilege if supplied to an expert for the purpose of preparing his expert report. (For more details on this point, see the consideration of the case above in the section entitled "Content, form and purpose of expert reports".) **11.016**

Abadeh v. British Telecommunications plc [2001] I.R.L.R. 23

In this case, the Employment Appeal Tribunal made some interesting comments about oral evidence from expert witnesses. **11.017**

The appellant worker was appealing against the decision of an employment tribunal that he was not disabled within the meaning of s.1(1) Disability Discrimination Act 1995.

The appellant obtained medical reports from Mr Nigel Padgham, a consultant ENT surgeon, and Dr Graham Rehlin, a consultant psychiatrist and psychotherapist. The respondent called Dr Diane Macaulay of the respondent's occupational health service, who was also the regional medical officer. The appellant received Dr Macaulay's first report two weeks before the tribunal hearing, and her additional report four days before the hearing.

The appellant decided, together with his union representative, to proceed on the basis of the written medical reports available to him, and not to call his experts to give oral evidence. The first instance employment tribunal thus only heard oral evidence from one medical witness, namely Dr Macaulay.

The Employment Appeal Tribunal held that the absence of any oral evidence from the appellant's doctors created a disadvantage both for the appellant and for the tribunal in dealing with the matter. However, the appellant made the decision not to seek to secure the attendance of his doctors, and could not later complain if the material before the tribunal was less than it should have been. The Employment Appeal Tribunal held that it was entirely proper for the tribunal to deal with the matter on the evidence presented to it, though it was incumbent upon it to consider and evaluate the contents of the written reports with care.

In relation to the evidence given by Dr Macaulay, the appellant complained that the tribunal relied on Dr Macaulay's evidence to such an extent that it allowed her to usurp its function of determining whether the appellant's ability to perform normal day-to-day activities had been substantially adversely affected. The appellant referred to the case of *Vicary v. British Telecommunications plc*

[1999] I.R.L.R. 680 in which Morison J. held that it is not the task of the medical expert to tell the tribunal whether or not impairments are substantial. That is the question which the tribunal itself has to answer. In the *Vicary* case, Morison J. said that the medical report should deal with the doctor's diagnosis of the impairments, the doctor's observation of the applicant carrying out day-to-day activities, and the ease with which he was able to perform those functions, together with any relevant opinion as to prognosis and the effect of medication. The Employment Appeal Tribunal noted that, coincidentally, *Vicary* involved the same respondent and also the same expert witness, Dr Macaulay. It held that it was satisfied that Dr Macaulay's report expressed opinions as to the application of the Disability Discrimination Act 1995, which were matters for the court rather than for her.

11.018   However, the question remained as to whether or not the tribunal decided the matter for themselves or whether they were unduly influenced by the expert witness. On the facts, the Employment Appeal Tribunal held that the tribunal was unduly persuaded by Dr Macaulay's assessment of whether or not the impairments were "substantial" under the Disability Discrimination Act 1995. The tribunal's conclusion that there was "no reason not to accept Dr Macaulay's evidence" was in any event looking at the matter the wrong way round. It suggested undue reliance upon Dr Macaulay's evidence and her assessment of the evidence.

In conclusion, as the Employment Appeal Tribunal concluded in the case of *Vicary*, the tribunal was satisfied that the first tribunal misdirected itself in law in the way it dealt with the expert evidence.

11.019   **Comment:**   This case is a reminder to inferior tribunals that they should not over-rely on evidence from expert witnesses. It is also another example of a tribunal indicating that it would have preferred to receive oral evidence from expert witnesses.

Kapadia v. Lambeth London Borough Council [2000] I.R.L.R. 699

11.020   This case is considered in the section above entitled "Duties of experts"; however, it also raises interesting issues relating to the use of expert evidence by the court in employment cases.

FIRE/EXPLOSION

Chappell v. Imperial Design Ltd (October 31, 2000) New Law 2001119701

11.021   This case before the Court of Appeal (Potter, Hale and Arden L.JJ.) turned on whether the first instance judge had erred in finding the claimant guilty of contributory negligence in view of his age.

The claimant was 13 at the time of an accident involving flammable vapour, which he found in a container left outside the defendant's factory. The first instance judge had assessed contributory negligence at 70 per cent. However, on appeal, the claimant argued that in performing the broad balancing exercise, the judge left two essential matters out of account. First, the negligence of the defendant in this case was to fail to provide against the very danger which occurred and which it recognised it was essential to guard against if harm to others, and in particular harm to children, was to be avoided. Second — and this is the element which is of interest to experts — when looking at the degree of contributory negligence to be attributed to the claimant, the judge failed to refer to the fact that the operative cause of the injuries to the claimant was not simply playing with fire. Instead, it was a phenomenon of which the claimant was entirely ignorant, namely the explosive mixture of air and vapour which might occur within the container which he was wielding. As explained to the Court of Appeal by the expert witness, and as was accepted throughout by the parties, there was no reason why the 13-year-old claimant should have antici-pated an explosion at all.

The Court of Appeal accepted these arguments and in its judgment instead apportioned on a 50/50 basis. Each of the judges referred to the expert report. Arden L.J. in particular, noted that the expert explained that even adults are frequently unaware of the explosive hazards of flammable liquids. She was also persuaded by the fact that the expert was not challenged on this point in cross-examination at the trial. She concluded by saying that the judge in this case misapprehended the relevance of the degree to which the claimant should have understood the risk of an explosion. The Court of Appeal could therefore, "review the apportionment itself to take account of this factor; and because [the expert's] report was not challenged on this particular point, it is an exercise which this court can perform for itself".

Comment: This case emphasises the importance that an expert report   **11.022**
can have when the Court of Appeal is deciding whether to substitute its own apportionment of liability between the parties. The expert report in this case was highly persuasive for the Court of Appeal.

INTELLECTUAL PROPERTY

Thermos Ltd v. Aladdin Sales [2000] F.S.R. 402

In this case, Jacob J. considered what expert evidence was legitimate in registered   **11.023**
design actions in view of the spirit and effect of the CPR. Interestingly, the action was commenced prior to the CPR coming into force and, as a result, each party had pre-pared, with the court's permission, expert reports. Jacob J. was of the view, however, that expert evidence was unnecessary. This case provides useful guidance as to what constitutes relevant expert evidence in the context of such actions.

Thermos had manufactured a vacuum flask, the design of which they had reg-istered. Aladdin had manufactured a two-cup "insulated" vacuum flask which Thermos claimed was an infringement of its design. Each party suggested that experts would be able to assist the court concerning technical matters and pro-duced expert evidence on that basis.

Jacob J. noted that each party had prepared witness statements and expert reports in the manner which had been conventional in registered design cases for many years. He considered that this had been of very little use in view of the fact that most registered designs were for consumer articles (*i.e.* objects bought or to be appreciated by ordinary members of the public). In this context he referred back to views he had expressed in *Isaac Oren v. Red Box Toy Factory Ltd* [1999] F.S.R. 785 which stand as a warning for lawyers:

"I do not think generally speaking, that "expert" evidence of this opinion sought (i.e. as to what ordinary consumer would see) in cases involving registered designs for consumer products is ever likely to be useful. There is a feeling amongst lawyers that one must always have an expert, but this is not so. No-one should feel that their case might be disadvantaged by not having an expert in an area where expert evidence is unnecessary. Evidence of technical or factual matters, as opposed to consumer "eye appeal" may, on the other hand, sometimes have a part to play — that would be to give the court information or understanding which it could not provide itself."

Jacob J. considered that the spirit of the CPR required the court to look even more closely at the need for expert evidence. He felt that, in registered design actions, the court should take care before allowing any expert evidence and should know precisely to which areas that expert evidence would be directed. If blanket permission was given, each side would feel compelled to get an expert who would have to say something. What would be said would then have to be read by the other side; and time and costs would be expended to no particular use. As to the question of whether an expert might be able to assist him about technical matters in the particular case at hand, Jacob J. considered that "this is so obvious that one hardly needs an expert, and certainly one does not need two experts". He therefore felt that the expert evidence in this case was completely redundant.

11.024   **Comment:**   This is a clear example of the effect of the CPR on expert evidence. The courts are as a result much more prepared to consider what is strictly necessary in terms of expert evidence. This case provides useful specific guidelines as to what expert evidence may be considered necessary in the context of registered design cases. A simple test to apply would be whether the courts need assistance in terms of information or understanding.

Rohm & Haas Co v. Collag Ltd [2001] F.S.R. 426

11.025   In this case, the claimant alleged that a process used by the defendant infringed its patent. The facts of the case are complex and technical, but the two main issues before Neuberger J. were: (a) the meaning of "surfactant" in the relevant process; and (b) whether the defendant's process infringed the claimant's patent.

At the end of a lengthy judgment, Neuberger J. held that on the basis that the reference to "one or more surfactants" in the patent in suit was to one or more amphiphiles, the defendant's process did not infringe the claimant's patent.

In coming to this conclusion, Neuberger J. relied heavily on expert evidence. This is interesting in itself because, as noted in his judgment, "in many, indeed most, cases of construction of a patent, expert evidence is not admissible". In this case, however, Neuberger J. admitted expert evidence from two expert witnesses for the claimant and two expert witnesses for the defendant. The reason for this was that the word in question, "surfactant", has a technical meaning.

Having decided the issue of admissibility, the judge's evaluation of the expert evidence was affected by which expert was closest to the addressee of the patent in suit. Having come to the conclusion that the patent in suit was addressed to a formulation scientist in the agrochemical field, he decided that, of the four expert witnesses from whom he had heard, Mr Knowles, called by the defendant, was the closest to the notional addressee of the patent in suit. He was also influenced by the fact that Mr Knowles' evidence was:

> "internally consistent, as well as being consistent with the evidence as a whole . . . his demeanour in the witness box and the way in which he dealt with the questions put to him did nothing to displace my impression that he was a witness who was doing his best to help the court rather than his client".

On the first issue, therefore, Neuberger J. relied on Mr Knowles' evidence that the "surfactant" would be understood to be referring to an amphiphile. Having decided the first issue, Neuberger J. came to the conclusion that the defendant's process did not infringe the claimant's patent.

Comment: This case is a useful reminder that in some circumstances,   11.026
expert evidence will be admissible in cases of construction of a patent. Indeed, once the expert evidence has been admitted, it is likely that a judge will rely heavily on such evidence. This is particularly the case if, as in this case, the judge comes to the conclusion that the expert witness "is doing his best to help the court rather than his client".

MEDICAL

Alexander v. Midland Bank Plc (1999) I.R.L.R. 723

This was a personal injury case in which the Court of Appeal (Stuart–Smith   11.027
and Buxton L.JJ. and Rattee J.) considered expert evidence in order to assess whether the claimants' injuries were physical or psychosomatic/psychogenic.

The claimants were employed by the defendant bank for a period of time as encoders. The sole function of the encoders was the rapid recording of the details of each cheque or voucher transaction passing through the centre. The gist of the claimants' complaints was that as a result of that work they suffered musculo-skeletal injury to their necks, arms and hands due to the rapid repetitive work.

There were four principal issues which the judge considered at the initial trial:

- the regime: this involved a consideration of the working conditions;

- the medical question: it was common ground that the claimants were suffering from fibro-myalgia and that this was work-related. This condition is now referred to as work-related upper-limb disorder ("WRULD") whereas previously it was known as repetitive strain injury ("RSI"). The dispute arose as to the basis of the condition. The claimants' case was that the condition was physical and amounted to a physical injury, although the precise aetiology of the condition was not known. The defendant's case was that it was not physical, but psychosomatic or psychogenic;

- causation: this was largely determined by the judge's findings on the first two issues; and

- the defendant's knowledge of the risk.

Under the regime heading, the judge made a careful assessment of the elements highlighted by the ergonomists. Mr Coleman appeared on behalf of the claimants. The substance of his evidence was that the causes of WRULD were multi-factorial, but the features that he criticised could lead to physical injury. Mr Pearce, for the defendant, on the other hand, was an exponent of the psychogenic school of thought. Logically, therefore, it would seem that the working condition could have little or no bearing on the condition.

11.028   On the second issue, of whether fibro-myalgia was a physical or a psychological condition, the principal witness for the claimants was Dr Mowatt, Honorary Senior Clinical Lecturer in Rheumatology at the University of Oxford and past president of the British Society of Rheumatology. Dr Mowatt's view was that there was a high probability that there was a single cause affecting all the claimants and that this was work-related. The judge's assessment of Dr Mowatt was that although he was perhaps the least fluent of the witnesses, he was:

> "Considerate, careful and conscientious as a witness, he was ready and fair in making concessions where he thought it right. He was realistic and frank . . . about the limitation of what he could specifically prove, but plainly he was honest in his conviction when he said that after all his examinations and the considerations he had given the cases, it was common sense which for him clinched the argument in the claimants' favour."

On the second issue, the judge also received evidence from Mr Varan, a Consultant Head Surgeon at the Black Rock Clinic in Dublin. He accepted that the claimants were suffering from fibro-myalgia and that their complaints were genuine and not exaggerated. However, he criticised Dr Mowatt's opinion on the ground that a patho-physiological explanation could not be given and that the diagnosis should not be made in the absence of physical signs. He said that if he could find no reasonable physical signs or pathology in the course of examination or in a patient's medical records, he diagnosed their problem as psychosomatic.

The judge commented that it seemed strange that in view of the fact that an important part of the debate was whether the claimants were exhibiting purely psychosomatic symptoms, neither party called a witness with psychiatric qualifications. The judge commented that none of the experts were qualified to give expert evidence in that field, even though for practical purposes connected with their own practice they might have seemed so qualified. The judge was also of the view that Mr Varan did not have the qualifications to express an expert's view in a legal forum about the psychological conclusions reached on the Australian epidemic and referred to in the related literature or to apply those conclusions to the individual claimants. The judge rejected Mr Varan's evidence that the claimants might be psychologically vulnerable to the extent that outside factors in their environment might induce in them psychosomatic disorders. In conclusion, the judge accepted the evidence of the claimants' expert that the condition was caused by the factors of repetitive work under intensive pressure with insufficient work breaks and sustained bad posture.

The defendant appealed, on the basis that: 11.029

- the judge had reversed the burden of proof and ought to have concluded that the claimants had not discharged the burden of proof; and

- the judge was not entitled to consider first whether the condition was likely to be psychogenic.

The Court of Appeal found that the judge was fully entitled to prefer the claimants' medical evidence. On the evidence:

> "There was a clear choice between two alternative explanations . . . the claimants had to prove that the physical explanation was more probable than the psychogenic one. The judge clearly had to weigh the strength of the psychogenic case before he reached a conclusion. It cannot matter in the least which he considers first."

The Court of Appeal found that there was no need to reject a physical cause where a number of honest and reliable witnesses, including the claimants, described broadly similar symptoms which were temporarily related to their work. The questions of posture and hours of work were interdependent in the sense that if there had been sufficient breaks the posture of the arm would have been of no consequence. Once criticisms of the workplace regime were established and it was known that such conditions could give rise to such complaints, it was more likely that the fibro-myalgia was physically based. The Court of Appeal found that:

> "The fallacy of the defendant's position is to assume that because the precise physical, pathological and anatomical explanation cannot as yet be explained, the condition must be all in the mind. I can see no basis for such presumption. . . ."

Comment: The main interest of this case lies in its particular subject   11.030
matter which is how the court will treat personal injury claims relating to WRULDs and more generally in relation to injuries which have no clear anatomical causes or causes which cannot as yet be verified.

Penney v. East Kent Health Authority [2000] Lloyd's Rep. Med. 41

In this case, the Court of Appeal (Lord Woolf M.R. and May and Hale L.JJ.)   11.031
considered whether the defendant cytoscreeners were justified in treating abnormalities on smear tests as innocuous, thereby returning negative results.

The actions arose out of cervical smears taken from the three claimants in the years 1989, 1990 and 1992. Each of the four smears was reported by the screeners as being negative. The consequence of the negative reports was that there was no timely follow-up and each of the subjects went on to develop invasive adenocarcinoma of the cervix.

The parties provided virtually no evidence of the actual training provided to the primary screeners. Instead, they put before the judge a general report which provided background information for the purposes of the case. The report was prepared in a collaborative effort by experts on both sides. The claimants produced a further report which was prepared as a result of an enquiry carried out by Sir William Wells, Chief Executive of the South Thames Region of the NHS. This report contained a catalogue of serious criticisms of the hospital. The Court of Appeal described this second report as

> "not irrelevant but of limited significance to the decisions to which the judge had to come on the issues which he had to determine. It was not more than part of the background against which he had to judge the evidence".

The judge heard evidence from five expert witnesses. The judge found that all five pathologists who gave evidence before him were doctors of distinction. He also found that they "gave their evidence with complete integrity and in a genuine attempt to assist the court". The approach of the experts was to give their opinion, based on their respective interpretation of what was on the slide, on the general question of whether a reasonably competent screener, exercising the appropriate standard of care, could treat the slide as negative.

The judge held that a reasonably competent screener would not have treated the slides in question as negative.

11.032   The appellants challenged the judge's decision on the question of the relevant state of knowledge at the time when each of the slides was reported and for not giving detailed reasons in his judgment for rejecting the appellants' case as to the state of knowledge. Further, the judge was criticised for deciding matters of opinion as if they were questions of fact (with specific regard to the state of knowledge).

The Court of Appeal was of the view that the question of what was known at the time of examination of the slides was only partially a question of fact. The state of knowledge may be objectively discernible and could, therefore, be a matter of fact. However, there would be room for differences of opinion as to the extent to which screeners at a particular time would be required to be aware of the latest learning on a particular subject.

One side was particularly difficult to interpret. The judge's approach was in effect to ask himself could a reasonably competent screener pass the slide as negative. Basing himself on his findings as to the abnormalities the slides showed, he considered it was not possible for the reasonably competent screener to do otherwise than to take the safe course and not trust the slide as negative.

The Court of Appeal was of the view that, to come to such a decision, it was not necessary to make a detailed analysis of the state of knowledge of the screeners in 1993. On that basis, the grounds of appeal of the health authority fell away.

The Court of Appeal then examined the findings in relation to the other smear tests. For each of those, the experts were divided as to the interpretation of the slides. Generally in those cases, the judge considered that the cytoscreener, having identified the abnormal cells, should have referred the slides on for further examination.

In the context of one of the slides, the Court of Appeal commented that "the evidence justified a finding that the slide showed clear abnormalities and the very disagreement between the experts underlined the fact that no primary cytoscreener could treat the abnormalities as innocuous". The Court of Appeal upheld the judge's findings. It was of the view that the approach of the judge was logical and that in any event the judge was in a better position than the Court of Appeal to assess the expert evidence. On that basis, the Court of Appeal considered that the judge was entitled to come to the conclusions which he did.

An additional point to note is that the judge had decided to allow evidence to be given of the results of examination of the slides which one of the experts had arranged to be carried out by cytoscreeners at his laboratory. There were a number of deficiencies in this exercise and the judge, in making the ruling that the evidence could be admitted, accepted that its evidential value was very seriously diminished. He thought that it was of "fringe relevance". The Court of Appeal was of the view that although careful attention had to be paid to its deficiencies, the evidence could not be said to be inadmissible. It was of some weight and of some support to the claimant's case and therefore the approach of the judge was the correct one.

Comment: The Court of Appeal endeavoured to clarify the significance   11.033
of their judgment in this case by emphasising that it related only to the particular slides which were the subject of the claim.

As to the approach of the judge in dealing with conflict between expert evidence, perhaps the best summary of the Court of Appeal's approach is its reference to the judgment of Bingham L.J. in *Eckersley v. Binnie* (1988) 18 Con.
L.R. 1 which set out guidance in this regard:

> "In resolving conflicts of expert evidence, the judge remains the judge; he
> is not obliged to accept evidence simply because it comes from an illustri-
> ous source; he can take account of demonstrated partisanship and lack of
> objectivity. But, save where an expert is guilty of a deliberate attempt to
> mislead (as happens only very rarely), a coherent reasoned opinion
> expressed by a suitably qualified expert should be the subject of a coherent
> reasoned rebuttal, unless it can be discounted for other good reason."

Matthews v. East Suffolk Health Authority (February 25, 2000) unreported

This case before the Court of Appeal (Henry and Robert Walker L.JJ. and   11.034
Alliott J.) was a medical negligence claim in which the issue was whether the
judge had been right to prefer the expert evidence of the defendant to that of
the claimant.

The claim arose from the care of the claimant shortly after her birth in
August 1982. She was born the elder of identical twins. As a result of the events
at her birth, she suffered from cerebral palsy and was severely disabled. One of
the key questions was when the brain damage had occurred and whether an earlier administration of antibiotics would have prevented it. As the case was tried
about sixteen years after the event, the court did not have the benefit of the rec-
ollection of witnesses to the events leading up to and after the birth. The court

had to rely on contemporaneous medical records and the analysis of those records by six expert medical witnesses.

The defendant adduced the evidence of Professor Wigglesworth, a professor in perinatal pathology at Hammersmith Hospital. He first identified in his statement periventricular leucomalacia ("PVL") as the cause of the brain damage. PVL was ultimately accepted by all experts as being the cause of the brain damage.

The judge preferred Professor Wigglesworth's evidence. One of the elements he took into account was that Professor Wigglesworth's expertise was pathology and that no other expert in this case possessed similar expertise. The judge therefore accepted Professor Wigglesworth's evidence that the episode at 12 o'clock marked the time at which the brain damage occurred. This was on the basis that he could not be satisfied on the balance of probabilities that the evidence established the occurrence of any brain damage at a later time. He did not consider therefore that the earlier administration of antibiotics would on the balance of probabilities have made a material difference.

The Court of Appeal's view was that the basic principles applying to appeals of this kind was that it should re-hear the case. However, the court considered that the judge was at an advantage in having heard the evidence and the challenges, referred to the decision in *Wilshire v. Essex Area Health Authority* [1988] 1 A.C. 1074 to the effect that:

> "Where expert witnesses are radically at issue about complex technical questions within their own field and are examined and cross-examined at length about their conflicting theories, I believe that the judge's advantage in seeing them and hearing them is scarcely less important than when he has to resolve some conflict of primary fact between lay witnesses in purely mundane matters".

11.035   One of the attacks made by the claimant was in relation to the qualifications of Professor Wigglesworth. The complaint was that, as a pathologist not claiming to be an expert in the clinical course of infectious diseases in living patients, his evidence should be in some way downgraded. The Court of Appeal commented that this was a point which was aired before the judge who dismissed it. The Court of Appeal considered that Professor Wigglesworth's expert evidence was clearly admissible and relevant and that the weight to be given to it was a matter for the judge. The judge was entitled to give it great weight if he chose to.

A factor which the Court of Appeal took into consideration in coming to its decision was that the claimant was required to show on the balance of probabilities that prompt application of antibiotics at noon or soon thereafter, would have avoided or quantifiably reduced the injuries caused by the brain damage. In the Court of Appeal's judgment this was not proven by the claimant's expert evidence or otherwise.

11.036   **Comment:**   The key in this case seemed to be that the burden of proof had not been discharged by the claimant. This case shows that the Court of Appeal will be reluctant to intervene to overturn findings of a trial judge based on expert evidence which the Court of Appeal has not heard and which the judge has heard.

Dingley v. Chief Constable of Strathclyde Police 2000 S.C. (H.L.) 77

This is the only case raising expert evidence issues which has come before the **11.037** House of Lords in the first two years since the implementation of the CPR. The issue before the House of Lords (Lord Browne Wilkinson, Lord Nicholls, Lord Steyn, Lord Hope and Lord Clyde) was the approach the court should take to competing expert evidence in a complex medical case.

The appellant was a retired officer. In the course of his employment as a constable, he was injured in a road accident. In the accident, he struck his head and suffered a whiplash injury to his neck. Seventeen days later, he started to develop the symptoms of multiple sclerosis ("MS"). He was retired from the force as his condition deteriorated. He took proceedings and the defendant admitted liability for the accident. The issue at trial was whether the trauma suffered in the accident had resulted in the development of MS. There was agreement between the parties' experts that trauma never caused the disease. The dispute was, however, as to whether trauma could trigger it.

This question was to be determined on the balance of probabilities. In this context, the House of Lords drew a distinction between "the exacting standards of thought and analysis which the academic will expect of medical scientists and the task of a judge when he is considering whether the essential elements in a pursuer's case have been established on a balance of probabilities".

In this context, the House of Lords was of the view that the role of the **11.038** expert witness is to give evidence. The judge's role was then to identify the real issues in the case and to determine where the balance lay between the competing positions revealed by the evidence on each side. In this context, an important part of the judge's task was to assimilate and understand the oral and written evidence and to penetrate the arguments developed by the expert witnesses. The House of Lords referred, in this context, to a statement made by Lord President Cooper in *Davie v. Magistrates of Edinburgh* 1953 S.C. 34: "expert witnesses, however skilled or eminent, can give no more than evidence. They cannot usurp the functions of the jury or judge sitting as a jury, anymore than a technical assessor can substitute his advice for the judgment of the court." The function of a judge in a civil case is to decide where the truth lies or whether the case has been made out, on a balance of probabilities. The House of Lords however considered that there was a risk that:

> "By immersing himself in every detail and by looking deeply into the minds of the experts, a judge may be seduced into a position where he applies to the expert evidence the standards which the expert himself will apply to the question whether a particular thesis has been proved or disproved — instead of assessing, as a judge must do, where the balance of probabilities lies on a review of the whole of the evidence."

The case includes a very detailed analysis of the evidence which was presented in this case and also provides comments on the different types of evidence and the weight that should be given to different items. In the context of published material, the view of the Court of Appeal was that a judge was entitled to proceed upon the basis that the calculations and conclusions be accepted for what they were worth, unless they were shown to be unsatisfactory by contrary evidence.

With regards to evidence of animal experiments, the House of Lords commented that:

> "There was an acute conflict between the experts as to the bearing which the experiments on animals had on the question of whether trauma can cause the onset of MS in humans. Animals do not develop MS and the condition from which they suffer, known as experimental allergic encephalitis, is not the same as MS. The weight to be attached to these experiments is a question on which views may differ among experts, but in a civil proof this is a matter for decision by the judge on a balance of probabilities."

The House of Lords' conclusion was that a satisfactory explanation would go a long way to supporting the appellant's case. However, the evidence did not go far enough to provide that explanation. Therefore the appellant's case failed on the balance of probabilities.

11.039   **Comment:**   This case is interesting in the detail of the expert evidence provided in the attempts by the appellant to show that symptomatic MS can be triggered by trauma and, in particular, a whiplash injury. There is also significant commentary on the interaction between the scientific standards being applied in order to prove a case and those applied by a judge, based on the balance of probabilities.

PERSONAL INJURY

Dyson v. Leeds City Council [2000] C.P. Rep. 42

11.040   This case before the Court of Appeal (Lord Woolf M.R. and Ward and Laws L.JJ.) is a further example of a challenge based on a judge's failure to give reasons as to why he preferred one expert's evidence over the evidence of another.

The action was commenced by the claimant as executor of Laurence Twohey, who died from mesothelioma due to exposure to asbestos. The relevant period for the purpose of the appeal was from May 1954 until July 1968. During that time, the deceased was employed as a plumber and heating engineer by a company. That company had a contract with the defendant for the service and maintenance of their heating boiler at a number of their premises.

The principal issue in the case was whether the defendant, as occupier of property, should have realised and taken precautions against asbestos dust in the 1950s (as contended by the claimant's expert) or by the 1970s (as contended by the defendant's expert).

The judge's findings were set out in a very short judgment. He stated:

> "Both experts . . . agreed that knowledge of the dangers of asbestos came first to the manufacturers of asbestos, secondly to major users of it such as the Royal Navy, then handlers of it such as employers and heating engineers and their employers, then occupiers of premises where asbestos had

been used for insulation or fire prevention purposes and finally the general public. I am bound to say that at the end of the day I found the evidence of Mr O'Neill (the defendant's expert) more persuasive than that of Mr Beauchamp (the claimant's expert) and that the time when a reasonable occupier would be aware of the need for steps to be taken to reduce the inhalation of asbestos dust would be the 1970s."

The judge went on to find in favour of the defendant. The major attack on his judgment was that he gave no reasons for preferring the evidence of the defendant's expert, Mr O'Neill.

The Court of Appeal commented that the judge had heard the experts over several hours giving their evidence and giving reasons as to why each held the opinion which he did. It was therefore intellectually possible to explain what it was about the evidence of Mr O'Neill that rendered his opinion more persuasive than that of Mr Beauchamp. However, the judge gave no intellectual reason for making the preferential decision he did. The Court of Appeal therefore considered that they were now "left in the unsatisfactory position of having disputed evidence, which is not necessarily so compelling on one side or the other, that we can properly substitute our judgment for that of the judge". On that basis, the only acceptable solution was for the case to be sent back for a further hearing.

Comment: This case is a reminder that judges must give adequate reasons for preferring the evidence of one expert over the evidence of another. The consequence of the judge not doing so in this case was quite serious in terms of cost and delay since the matter had to be re-heard. **11.041**

Indeed, in a case a few months before the CPR came into force, the Court of Appeal (Henry and Laws L.JJ. and Hidden J.) went to the trouble of setting out guidance on the giving of reasons by judges. In this case — *Flannery v. Halifax Estate Agencies Limited* [2000] 1 W.L.R. 377 — the court said that the first instance judge's failure to give reasons for a conclusion was, of itself, a good ground of appeal. The court ordered a new trial for the case. The Court of Appeal went on to give useful guidelines on the duty of judges to give reasons.

- The duty to give reasons is a function of due process, and therefore of justice. Its rationale has two principal aspects. The first is that fairness requires that the parties should be left in no doubt why they have won or lost. This is especially so since without reasons the losing party will not know whether the court has misdirected itself, and thus whether he may have an available appeal on the substance of the case. The second aspect is that a requirement to give reasons concentrates the mind; if it is fulfilled, the resulting decision is much more likely to be soundly based on the evidence than if it is not.

- The first of these aspects implies that want of reasons may be a good self-standing ground of appeal.

- The extent of the duty, or rather the reach of what is required to fulfil it, depends on the subject-matter. Where there is a straightforward factual dispute whose resolution depends simply on which witness is telling the truth about events which he claims to recall, it is likely to be enough for the judge to indicate simply that he believes X rather than Y. However, where the dispute involves something in the nature of an intellectual exchange, with reasons and analysis advanced on either side, the judge must enter into the issues canvassed before him and explain why he prefers one case over the other.

- This is not to suggest that there is one rule for cases concerning witnesses' truthfulness or recall of events, and another for cases where the issue depends on reasoning or analysis (with experts or otherwise). The rule is the same: the judge must explain *why* he has reached his decision. The question is always: what is required of the judge to do so? That will differ from case to case. Transparency should be the watchword.

Coker v. Barkland Cleaning Co. (December 6, 1999) unreported

11.042   In this personal injury case before the Court of Appeal (Swinton Thomas and May L.JJ.), the court considered which medical expert evidence was to be preferred in relation to a back injury sustained by the claimant.

The claimant was employed by the defendant as a cleaner at a Tesco supermarket. Whilst he was working he was struck from behind by a cleaning machine. The judge found that the defendant was liable for the accident. The primary issue in relation to damages was the extent to which the accident was the cause of the claimant's disabilities in view of the fact that he had a pre-existing disability in his back.

The consultant orthopaedic surgeon called on behalf of the claimant, Mr Baker, attributed the symptoms from which the claimant was suffering to the accident on the basis that there was no inevitability that the claimant's back problem was going to deteriorate. In contrast, Mr Unwin, on behalf of the defendant, considered that the symptoms from which the claimant was suffering were not a result of the accident, but from his pre-existing disability.

The judge preferred the evidence of Mr Unwin to that of Mr Baker, finding that as a matter of probability the symptoms from which Mr Coker was suffering did result from the pre-existing disability. However, he then went on to make a finding that Mr Coker's symptoms had been exacerbated for a period of two years as opposed to Mr Unwin's maximum of one year.

On appeal, the claimant submitted that it was not open to the judge to reach the conclusion that he did. There was also a cross-appeal by the defendant on the basis that once the judge had accepted Mr Unwin's evidence as a matter of generality, he had no evidential basis for extending the period of acceleration from 12 months to two years.

The Court of Appeal decided that the judge was not plainly wrong. He was therefore entitled to prefer the evidence of Mr Unwin to that of Mr Baker.

The Court of Appeal went on to consider the cross-appeal. The Court of Appeal found that the judge was "plainly entitled to take into account the evidence that he had heard from Mr Baker and he was entitled to take the view that Mr Unwin's maximum of 12 months was, on the totality of the evidence, too short a time, and that a somewhat longer period of exacerbation was more likely". The Court of Appeal considered that a period of two years was on all the evidence a reasonable assessment.

A separate issue was raised in relation to engineering expert evidence obtained for the case. The only witness to the accident was the person in charge of the cleaning machine. He made a statement to the claimant's solicitors in which he said that he let go of the machine and turned away to do something else and the machine "ran away". He then made a statement through the defendant's solicitors in which he said that he was in charge of the machine throughout. As a result, both sets of advisors thought that it was necessary to obtain expert evidence on the issue. This turned out to be a fruitless exercise in the sense that it became evident that the witness was in charge of the machine at all times and that the claimant was bound to succeed in establishing liability.

The Court of Appeal was not impressed by the amount of costs incurred in relation to the engineering investigation. May L.J. stated that:

> "A forthright look by both sides at the only real liability issue in this case shows, and would have shown, that if indeed Mr Coker was hit from behind by the cleaning machine there was no viable defence on liability. It did not matter whether this was because someone was driving the machine or because it moved without a driver."

As a result, May L.J. stated that the parties should early on have focused on the real liability issues. May L.J. stressed the need for parties to co-operate in order to avoid this kind of unnecessary expense:

> "Modern litigation culture and Part 1 of the Civil Procedure Rules requires the parties to help the court to further the overriding objective. This requires the parties to co-operate with the court and with each other to avoid unnecessary expense. In the present case sensible co-operation did not achieve the saving of expense which is now the subject of the cost debate."

Comment: This case clearly emphasises the need for parties to co-operate   11.044
in order to avoid unnecessary costs in instructing experts. In addition, it highlights how a judge can substitute his own assessment, even where he has agreed with the general principles of one party's expert evidence.

Hill v. Durham County Council (January 31, 2000) unreported

The issue before the Court of Appeal (Stuart-Smith and Sedley L.JJ.) in this   11.045
personal injury case was whether a recorder had given sufficient reasons for preferring the evidence of one expert.

The claimant was employed by the defendant as a teacher at a primary school. In dance training, the claimant ruptured her Achilles tendon. The claimant's claim was that the dance teacher employed by the defendant, a Mrs Redfearn, had failed to enquire whether the participants were accustomed to taking exercise and had adopted an unsuitable warm-up procedure which was too vigorous. The recorder rejected both grounds.

In his judgment, the recorder had summarised briefly the view of the claimant's expert, Miss Rist, that the exercise was an unsuitable system of warm-up. Mrs Redfearn's evidence as to the suitability of the system of warm-up was not dealt with in the judgment at all, save only in the conclusions to which the recorder came, as follows:

"The evidence I have heard has indicated that warm-up exercises can never completely prevent injuries from taking place and I do not find that there was a foreseeable risk that this injury would have occurred on this occasion. I do not find that the train game was an inappropriate way to warm up having made the findings that I have set out in this judgment."

The claimant appealed on the basis that the recorder had failed to give reasons for preferring the evidence of Mrs Redfearn to that of the claimant's expert.

11.046   The Court of Appeal was of the view that the judgment of the recorder lacked reasoning, and that he should have said why he preferred the evidence of Mrs Redfearn:

"The recorder ought to have said in terms what he preferred as the description of what was, in effect, happening and that he accepted in terms that he preferred Mrs Redfearn's evidence that it was a suitable form of warm-up which had been conducted on many occasions by her, both with children and with adults."

However, the Court of Appeal did not consider that this was one of the cases where the reasoning behind the conclusion was so essential that the court should say that the matter could not stand. The recorder was entitled to conclude that the type of activity was an appropriate form of warm-up even for adults and this was one of those unfortunate accidents for which no-one was responsible.

11.047   **Comment:**   This is another reminder that judges will need to give reasons when distinguishing between expert evidence given for each party. In particular, they will need to specify why they preferred one source of evidence over another.

Huxley v. Elvicta Wood Engineering Ltd (April 19, 2000) unreported

11.048   In this case, the Court of Appeal (Kennedy, Buxton and Hale L.JJ.) held that the trial judge had been entitled to prefer the expert evidence of the claimant to that of the defendant.

The claimant began to work for the first defendant in 1954 as a machine operator. The claimant had been heavily exposed to wood dust. In May 1992 he was found to be suffering from sino-nasal cancer. At trial, the claimant contended that, at least on the balance of probabilities, it was wrongful exposure which caused his cancer.

Three expert witnesses were called: a Professor Seaton for the claimant, and a Mr Baer and a Dr Gallimore for the defendant. Professor Seaton, after many years as a consultant chest physician, had been specialising in recent years in the field of occupational health. Mr Baer had since 1993 been a consultant ENT surgeon and Dr Gallimore had since 1992 been Honouree Consultant Histopathologist at the Royal Free Hospital in London. Dr Gallimore examined a biopsy and provided evidence as to the nature of the claimant's condition which was not disputed. Professor Seaton and Mr Baer gave expert evidence which was intended to assist the judge in deciding whether, on the balance of probabilities, the claimant's condition was caused by his exposure to wood dust. Professor Seaton did not himself examine the claimant, but he and Mr Baer examined a number of studies reported in medical journals, and brought to bear their skill in interpreting those publications. Professor Seaton's conclusion was that on the balance of probabilities the exposure was causative in the case of an individual who (1) had had prolonged and heavy exposure, especially if that exposure had been to hardwood dust, and (2) had developed the tumour at a time consistent with the known natural history of carcinogenesis. Mr Baer's opinion was to the opposite effect.

The Court of Appeal noted that the skill which each expert brought to bear was his skill in sifting through and evaluating medical studies carried out by others, a skill which over the years Professor Seaton must have had to exercise more than the other expert witness. Furthermore, his experience was greater, having qualified in 1962, as against Mr Baer's qualification in 1981. The Court of Appeal mentioned these matters in their judgment because the trial judge had been criticised for preferring the evidence of Professor Seaton to that of Mr Baer. In what the Court of Appeal described as an "important" paragraph towards the end of his judgment, the judge said:

> "Professor Seaton was a most impressive witness of great experience and authority; he was candid in the views he expressed and gave his evidence in a detached and independent manner. He squarely faced up to the views raised by Mr Nixon in his very skilful and searching cross-examination. Although a detailed analysis of his reports were shown to point to some imprecision of language and he had not mentioned all the literature, his oral evidence to me was very clear, fair and objective; it had taken into account all the literature and other evidence available by the time of the trial. I preferred his evidence to that of Mr Baer who was far more heavily reliant on the published papers than his own experience. I accept Professor Seaton's conclusions on the evidence."

Counsel for the appellants submitted that the judge did not have sufficient regard for the relevant experience and expertise of the party's expert witnesses. The Court of Appeal said that if the experts misinterpreted the material with which they had to work, and in particular if they misinterpreted it for partisan reasons, then that would be bound to affect the judge's assessment of them. However, if they were each doing what they could, then it was impossible for the Court of Appeal to go behind the judge's evaluation of the expert witnesses and of the impact of their evidence.

In conclusion, the judge attached respective weight to the expert evidence because of what he rightly considered to be the most reliable expert evidence available to him. The appeal was therefore dismissed.

Comment: This case is a demonstration of the usual Court of Appeal   **11.049** practice of not interfering with case management decisions unless it is absolutely necessary. Nevertheless, the detailed reasoning of the Court of Appeal suggests that this was not a clear-cut decision.

Sandry v. Jones, The Times, **August 3, 2000**

11.050   In this case, the Court of Appeal (Swinton-Thomas, Brooke and Hale L.JJ.) made some interesting comments on what level of judicial expertise is required to try any case, in particular one involving conflicting expert evidence.

The claim arose as a result of a road traffic accident, when the defendant's car collided with the rear of the claimant's vehicle. In due course liability was admitted, with the result that the judge was only trying the issue of quantum.

The Court of Appeal noted that the case was, at least on the papers, a substantial claim which involved contested medical and accountancy issues. Swinton-Thomas L.J. in giving the leading judgment of the Court of Appeal, said that, unless there was some compelling reason why it was necessary for a particular case to be tried by a district judge, it was more appropriate that a case of this complexity should be tried by a circuit judge.

Another interesting aspect of this case is that both counsel drew the Court of Appeal's attention to the case of *Flannery v. Halifax Estate Agencies Limited* [2000] 1 W.L.R. 377. Although the facts of the case were very different to the facts of the present case, the judgment does have some relevance. The Court of Appeal referred to the following passage:

> ". . . a judge was under a duty to explain why he had reached his decision; that the scope of what was required to fulfil that duty depended on the subject matter of the case; that where reasons and analysis were advanced on either side a judge had to enter into issues canvassed and explain why he preferred one case over the other; that failure to supply reasons in those circumstances offended against requirements inherent in the duty of showing fairness to both parties and of producing a decision soundly based on the evidence and constituted a good free-standing ground of appeal; that, accordingly, since the judge heard reasoned analysis and accepted the defendants' expert evidence, he was under a duty to supply reasons in the form of a coherent rebuttal of the plaintiffs' expert evidence; and that his failure to do so justified setting aside his judgement and remitting the case for re-trial".

11.051   The Court of Appeal held that it seemed that if the judge was going to reject the claimant's claim for loss of earnings, based on his evidence that he was unable to continue with his business on account of his neck injury, it was incumbent upon the judge to deal with his reasons for rejecting that aspect of the claim with a degree of detail, supported by proper reasoning. For that reason, the Court of Appeal came to the conclusion that the case, on the issue of loss of earnings alone, had to be remitted for a re-trial.

Swinton-Thomas L.J. also held that he was minded to direct that the re-hearing should take place before a circuit judge who was experienced in trying personal injury actions. Brooke L.J. noted that the matter is governed by paragraph 12.10 of the Practice Direction to Part 26 of the CPR. This reads:

> "Unless the court otherwise directs, a Master or a District Judge may decide the amount payable under a relevant order irrespective of the financial value of the claim and of track to which the claim may have been allocated."

However, Brooke L.J. added that a procedural judge determining whether to direct pursuant to that Practice Direction should, in future, follow the guidance given in this case by the Court of Appeal.

Comment: This case is of interest to expert witnesses for two reasons.   11.052
First, experts may wish to be aware that if they are dealing with complex subjects, where their opinion conflicts with that of their counterparts, the guidance given in this case by Swinton-Thomas L.J. suggests that the issue of damages should be decided by a High Court judge or a circuit judge. Paragraph 12.10 of the Practice Direction to Part 26 should therefore now be interpreted in line with this case.

Second, it is a good reminder that a judge is required to give reasons why he prefers one set of expert evidence to another. The reasoning of the first instance judge in this case was not sufficient. The judge recognised that the experts in the case before him "differed significantly" and concluded that "on a balance of probabilities the claimant has not satisfied me that the loss of profit claim has been proved so far as giving up the "van" aspect of the business is concerned". The Court of Appeal held that the relevant paragraph in the judgment of the judge was "very inadequate".

Jones v. Wilkins, The Times, February 6, 2001

In an appeal on the apportionment of liability between joint tortfeasors, the   11.053
Court of Appeal (Nourse, Mummery and Keene L.JJ.) was assisted by evidence from an expert witness.

The claimant was a passenger in a vehicle that was involved in a collision with a vehicle driven by the defendant. At the time of the accident, the claimant was two years old and was sitting on her mother's lap in the front passenger seat. She was restrained by the lap strap of the seatbelt that went round both her and her mother. The diagonal strap went round the mother's body only. The claimant sued through her litigation friend for personal injury. The defendant admitted negligence but joined the mother and the driver as Part 20 defendants.

The expert witness, a Dr Rattenbury, said in his report that using one lap belt to restrain both an adult and a child is in fact the worst possible solution in terms of injuries to a child, worse even than having no belt around the child. However, his report concluded by stating that he was doubtful that the public as a whole was suf-ficiently well-informed about the risks of severe injury to a child carried in this way.

In assessing blameworthiness, the Court of Appeal noted Dr Rattenbury's comments that ordinary members of the public do not understand how dan-gerous it is to attempt to protect a child by putting an adult lap belt around a child. In his judgment, Keene L.J. said that in the light of this case, members of the public ought to be so advised and those responsible for road safety may wish to consider giving greater publicity to the risks attendant in this situation.

As things stood in this case, the blame to be attached to the mother and the driver had to be limited by their lack of understanding of this risk. This was a lack of understanding which they shared with much of the public and which in that sense was objectively understandable. Taking these and other factors into account, the Court of Appeal held that the judge's apportionment was not sus-ceptible to attack. One could not say that the trial judge was clearly wrong in apportioning 75 per cent of the liability to the defendant driver and 25 per cent to the mother and sister.

11.054   **Comment:**   This case is a good example of how the courts find expert evidence useful in deciding whether or not to disturb the trial judge's exercise of discretion. It is also an example of how experts can inform the court of facts which are so important that the court makes recommendations on the basis of the evidence that it hears.

Lougheed v. Safeway Stores plc [2001] **E.W.C.A. Civ. 176**

11.055   The Court of Appeal (Ward L.J. and Maurice Kay J.) held in this case that where the evidence of medical expert witnesses supported a claimant's allegation of chronic pain disorder, the Court of Appeal had no option but to overturn a judge's finding of fact that was inconsistent with the evidence.

The claimant worked for the respondent as a store supervisor. In July 1993 she slipped in the store and fractured her coccyx. In May 1997 she obtained a judgment against the respondent, with damages to be assessed. She was then examined by medical experts for both sides, including consultant orthopaedic surgeons, consultant psychiatrists and a consultant neuropsychologist. The issue was whether the claimant's ongoing pain was attributable to her accident.

The judge at first instance was not satisfied that the claimant had given a full and frank picture of her disability and held that it was likely that the accident was not the cause of the claimant's pain.

The Court of Appeal disagreed: on the agreed medical evidence, the claimant was in continuous pain. On the more difficult question of the claimant's credibility, the Court of Appeal said it had difficulty in understanding the inconsistency between the judge's finding that the claimant was a genuine person and his finding that she was not honest with the medical practitioners. The Court of Appeal noted that the experts had never doubted her honesty and were not challenged about this. Neither was the claimant challenged about it.

The court further held that the interests of justice were against a re-trial and in favour of the Court of Appeal deciding the outstanding issues. Accordingly, the Court of Appeal found that the claimant's chronic pain disorder was caused by the respondent's negligence.

11.056   **Comment:** This is yet another example which makes it clear that where a judge hears consistent evidence from expert witnesses, and chooses to reject their opinion, he must give very clear reasons in his judgment for doing so.

Holmes v. SGB Services plc (February 19, 2001) unreported

11.057   The issue before the Court of Appeal (Henry, Buxton and Arden L.JJ.) was whether the claimant should be allowed to amend his particulars of claim to plead a case put forward by a court-appointed expert.

The claimant alleged that he was injured through the fault of the defendant in October 1995. The defendant said that there was no objective evidence of the accident. Proceedings were commenced in October 1998. The trial date was set for September 2000. There was no application for expert evidence, which the claimant said was due to an oversight on his part. However, in the listing questionnaire filed in January 2000, the claimant did state that directions for expert evidence were required. In August 2000 a district judge made an order for expert evidence to be filed by a date shortly thereafter. The expert signed his report in

August 2000. The expert did not support the claimant's case, but suggested another possible case. The claimant made an application to vacate the date of the trial — set for three weeks later.

The judge at first instance allowed the claimant's application to amend his particulars of claim to plead the explanation postulated by the expert. Accordingly, he adjourned the trial. The judge said: **11.058**

> "As the engineer instructed jointly on the direction of the court was asked to answer questions provided by the court, and says in effect that he thinks he is being asked the wrong questions, it seems to me that in this case it is appropriate to allow the claimant to endeavour to investigate the alternative case postulated, but I have to say no more than postulated by the engineer."

The defendants complained in their appeal to the Court of Appeal, that the application to adduce expert evidence was made very late in the day and noted other factors relating to delay and expense. However, the Court of Appeal noted that the judge was exercising a discretion and making a case management decision. The defendant, therefore, had to show that the judge erred in principle, not simply that he could have reached some other decision. The Court of Appeal held that the judge correctly applied the overriding objective when he concluded that it was fair that the claimant should have the opportunity to amend his particulars and instruct the expert on further matters.

However, the Court of Appeal added a "rider"; Arden L.J. said that the claimant's evidence should be completed, if there was to be any more evidence from him, before the expert was given fresh instructions.

Comment: The Court of Appeal in this case followed its usual practice of   **11.059** not overruling a first instance judge's case management unless he erred in principle. However, as the Court of Appeal made quite clear, this case was "*distinctly unusual*". Firstly, the CPR only applied to the case late in the day. Secondly, and Buxton L.J. described this as an "oddity", the revised case was not thought up by the claimant himself or his advisers, nor was it even advanced by an expert instructed by him. It was instead suggested by the court-appointed expert. It is for this reason that we are unlikely to see such leniency in allowing the further instruction of experts in other cases. In this case, as the judge said himself, it would have been unusual and unsatisfactory to go forward to trial in circumstances where the sole expert witness, jointly instructed by both parties, was giving a possible explanation of the accident which was different from the one, that on the pleadings, had to be tried.

PLANNING

Motor Crown Petroleum Ltd v. S J. Berwin & Co. (a firm) [2000] Lloyd's Rep. P.N. 438

In this case, the issue before the Court of Appeal (Roch and Wood L.JJ. and   **11.060** Gage J.) was the judge's assessment of the likelihood of success of an appeal against a planning decision.

In 1991 the respondent company, which developed and operated petrol stations, applied for planning permission for a site in Hampshire. Permission was refused. The company retained the appellant solicitors to act for them in the appeal. The appellants were retained at the suggestion of the second defendant, a Mr Unwin. The appeal failed in 1992.

The respondent took proceedings claiming that the appellants should have advised a challenge to the local plan. The judge's findings were that the appellant should have advised the respondent to challenge the local plan and that such challenge would have been successful. As a consequence, the respondent's appeal against the refusal of their application for planning permission for their site would have been made in the context of a development plan in which the appeal site was not designated as coast and countryside. Such an appeal would have had a real or substantial chance of success. The judge assessed the chances of success of such an appeal to be 40 per cent.

11.061   One of the grounds of appeal by the solicitors was whether the judge's 40 per cent assessment of chance of success was correct. The appellant's principal criticism was in relation to the way the judge dealt with assessing the likelihood of success. In particular, they argued that the judge did not remind himself of the evidence of the three expert witnesses on this point. Neither did the judge attempt to analyse their evidence or, if he was rejecting the opinions of the experts, say why he was doing so.

The judge had heard three expert witnesses. The expert witness for the respondent had expressed the view that the chances of a planning appeal being allowed following a successful challenge to the local plan were 75 per cent. The appellant's expert concluded that whether or not a challenge had been mounted and, whatever the outcome of a challenge, the respondent company's appeal would have been dismissed. The second defendant's expert was of the view that a challenge to the local plan would have been unsuccessful and that therefore the appeal would have failed.

In holding that the judge had sufficiently expressed his assessment and the route by which he had arrived at that assessment, the Court of Appeal made relevant comments in relation to experts. The judge was not bound to choose between the opinions of the experts for the respondent and the appellants. In this regard, the Court of Appeal was of the view that:

> "The importance of the expert evidence was that it identified the factors which would have been in place in the hypothetical planning appeal which would have followed a successful challenge to the local plan" and that therefore "once the facts are found it is a question of an assessment which is to be made, not by experts, but by the judge."

What was important in this context was not minute examination of every detail but "a more general estimate of the chances of success".

11.062   **Comment:** This case serves to remind us of the purpose of expert evidence to identify relevant factors which come into play so that a judge can make an informed assessment. This case is also interesting on its particular facts in terms of estimating the chances of success of the appeal following successful amendment to the local plan.

Jolley v. Carmel Ltd [2000] E.G. 185

In this case before Mr Lewison Q.C., sitting as a Deputy High Court Judge, **11.063** the main issue was the nature of any implied term relating to obtaining planning permission.

He held that it was impossible to imply a term which imposed on a buyer an absolute obligation to obtain planning permission. A term should be implied that the buyer would make reasonable efforts to obtain the grant of planning permission within a reasonable time. However, the buyer would not be in breach of the implied term so long as any delay in obtaining planning permission was attributable to causes beyond its control. In any event, the expert evidence that he heard was that a reasonable time for obtaining planning permission would be 23 months, and that period had not yet elapsed.

Interestingly, the judge found useful expert evidence given on a hypothetical basis. Mr Macateer was an expert in planning and had been asked for his opinion on how long a hypothetical planning application would have taken. He accepted in cross-examination that he had not previously undertaken this exercise. However, the judge held that that did not cause him to doubt the expert's reliability, particularly since his conclusions were not seriously challenged. Furthermore, no contrary expert opinion evidence was called. The judge referred to Mr Macateer's evidence, which was that the planning application process, including either a call-in or an appeal, would have taken about 23 months. The judge concluded:

> "In my judgment the right approach is to join Mr Macateer's timetable at the point at which the planning application is made. The application for Scheme 1A was submitted in October 1998. Twenty months from that date have not yet elapsed. On that basis, therefore, the contract has not yet lapsed."

(The appeal against the judge's decision was dismissed by the Court of Appeal.)

Comment: One might think that expert evidence given on a hypothetical **11.064** basis would not be encouraged by the courts in the light of CPR r.35.1 and the court's duty to restrict expert evidence to that which is reasonably required to resolve the proceedings. However, the Court of Appeal noted, without criticism, the fact that the judge heard and considered expert evidence as to what would have been a reasonable period (viewed objectively and as the date of the contract) for obtaining planning permission at the requisite time. Indeed, it said that this "was necessary in case he was wrong in his primary conclusion".

PROFESSIONAL NEGLIGENCE

Michael Hyde & Associates Ltd v. JD Williams & Co. Ltd [2001] P.N.L.R. 233

In this case the issue before the Court of Appeal (Nourse, Ward and Sedley **11.065** L.JJ.) was a narrow area of dispute: was it sufficient for an architect to draw a client's attention to the risk of phenolic yellowing of textiles in their warehouse, or was it necessary for the architects to enquire further to establish how serious the risk was?

The judge at first instance reviewed the authorities on expert evidence and came to the conclusion that the authorities prevent a judge from deciding between two logically based expert opinions when the judge has no expertise in the field of those experts. However, where the issue does not in itself require any particular expertise, the authorities do not prohibit the judge from deciding the issue, notwithstanding the fact that experts have given evidence to the effect that each would have approached the matter in question in a different way. Having decided that the court did not need any expert help in this case, the judge decided that the defendant had overlooked a risk which it ought to have brought to the claimant's attention.

The Court of Appeal held that the judge approached the case in the wrong way. Ward L.J. said that as he read the evidence in this case, the experts were doing no more than putting themselves forward as reasonably competent architects, and then saying what they themselves would have done in the circumstances. In his judgment, this case could well have been decided and disposed of by adoption of the views of Oliver J. in *Midland Bank Trust Company Ltd v. Hett Stubbs and Kemp (a firm)* [1979] 1 Ch. 384:

> "Clearly, if there is some practice in the profession, some accepted standard of conduct which is laid down by a professional institute or sanctioned by common usage, evidence of that can and ought to be received. But evidence which really amounts to no more than an expression of opinion by a particular practitioner of what he thinks he would have done had he been placed, hypothetically and without the benefit of hindsight, in the position of the defendants, is of little assistance to the court. . . ."

11.066   Ward L.J. said that had the judge followed that course, it would have been very difficult to criticise him for it. In the view of the Court of Appeal, this case simply required the court to decide, with whatever help the expert evidence afforded, whether a competent architect could have overlooked the risk in issue of the disclaimer.

Nevertheless, although the judge employed different reasoning, the Court of Appeal held that he was entitled to decide the issue for himself and to come to the conclusion that he did. Although the Court of Appeal's reason for rejecting the defendant's argument was not quite the same as that of the judge, it also held that the defendant overlooked a real risk (referring to the case of *Nye Saunders and Partners v. Alan E. Bristow* (1987) 37 B.L.R. 92 which applied the *Bolam* [1957] 1 W.L.R. 582 test of negligence to architects).

11.067   **Comment:**   This Court of Appeal decision is interesting in that it gives guidance on how expert evidence should be used by the judge. In this case, the Court of Appeal was of the opinion that there was no need to inquire into competing schools of professional practice, *i.e.* the principle laid down in *Bolitho v. City of Hackney Health Authority* [1998] A.C. 232. In a case such as this, when a judge is faced with two responsible bodies of opinion, the judge should not simply decide which opinion to accept. The court should decide the issue for itself "with whatever help the expert evidence affords".

Calver v. Westwood Veterinary Group [2001] Lloyd's Rep. P.N. 102

In this case, the Court of Appeal (Simon Brown and Mummery L.JJ.) made **11.068** interesting comments on the approach the court should take when comparing the evidence of two experts. The Court of Appeal was clear that in some cases it is possible that both expert reports are capable of logical support, and that one body of professional opinion need not be condemned.

The case was a professional negligence action against a veterinary group. Mr Hughes, an experienced principal veterinary surgeon in the appellant group, had examined the respondent's mare, which had aborted overnight in a field. Having examined the mare, Mr Hughes decided not to conduct a uterine examination and, more particularly, not to administer prophylactic antibiotics.

At first instance, the judge determined that the vet had been negligent. The hearing before the judge lasted four days and a great deal of evidence was given. Most important for the purposes of the appeal was the evidence of three vets: Mr Hughes himself, Mr Greenwood (the appellant's expert) and Mr Vogel (the respondent's expert). The central difference between the experts lay in their attitude towards the administration of antibiotics.

Mr Vogel's approach was that all competent vets would be bound to administer antibiotics in any case where on examination the vet could not be 100 per cent sure that the whole of the placenta had been expelled, or where there was a possibility that the mare had aborted more than three hours before her abortion was discovered. Mr Hughes' and Mr Greenwood's opinion was to the contrary. Both thought it essential in each case for the examining vet to make a clinical judgement on whether the placenta was intact and the animal well before administering antibiotics. The judge at first instance preferred Mr Vogel's views as to the correct practice to be followed.

On appeal, it was the appellant's case, based on the evidence of Mr Greenwood and Mr Hughes, that neither uterine examination nor the administration of prophylactic antibiotics were appropriate. Unless that professional opinion could be shown to be plainly unreasonable in the sense of being incapable of withstanding logical analysis, the judge could not properly hold it to be negligent (*Bolam v. Frien Hospital Management Committee* [1957] 1 W.L.R. 583, as explained by the House of Lords in *Bolitho v. City and Hackney Health Authority* [1998] A.C. 232 applied).

The Court of Appeal agreed that, assuming the judge correctly applied *Bolitho*, he must be taken to have held that Mr Hughes' and Mr Greenwood's approach was incapable of withstanding logical analysis.

The Court of Appeal cited at length "critical" paragraphs from Lord Browne- **11.069** Wilkinson's speech in *Bolitho*:

> "In the vast majority of cases the fact that distinguished experts in the field are of a particular opinion will demonstrate the reasonableness of that opinion . . . but if, in a rare case, it can be demonstrated that the professional opinion is not capable of withstanding logical analysis, the judge is entitled to hold that the body of opinion is not reasonable or responsible."

> "I emphasise that in my view it will very seldom be right for a judge to reach the conclusion that views genuinely held by a competent medical expert are unreasonable."

"As the quotation from Lord Scarman makes clear, it would be wrong to allow such assessment to deteriorate into seeking to persuade the judge to prefer one of two views both of which are capable of being logically supported. It is only where a judge can be satisfied that the body of expert opinion cannot be logically supported at all that such opinion will not provide the benchmark by reference to which the defendant's conduct falls to be assessed."

The Court of Appeal said that this case comes down to the question whether the judge was entitled to regard this case as one of those "rare cases" in which one body of veterinary opinion (represented by Mr Vogel) demonstrated that the other (represented by Mr Hughes and Mr Greenwood) was not capable of withstanding logical analysis. The Court of Appeal held that it seemed impossible on the evidence to condemn the body of professional opinion represented by Mr Hughes and Mr Greenwood as illogical. It therefore held that the practice followed by Mr Hughes was not negligent.

11.070   **Comment:**   This is a salutary reminder to experts that their reports and opinions cannot form the basis of a finding of professional negligence unless the contrary opinion is not capable of withstanding logical analysis. As stated in the *Bolitho* case, in the "vast majority of cases" expert opinion will simply show the reasonableness of a defendant's opinion by the fact that it is shared by a distinguished expert in the field.

SEAMANSHIP

Owners of the ship "Pelopidas" v. Owners of the ship "TRSL Concord" (1999) 2 All E.R. (Comm) 737

11.071   The relevance of this case before Steel J. lies in its analysis of the extent to which seamanship evidence can be adduced in the context of ship collision cases.

The claimant's ship "Pelopidas" and the defendant's ship "TRSL Concord" collided in the access channel to Buenos Aires.

Both parties engaged the services of a wide range of experts with a view to apportioning each vessel's responsibility for the collision. In the event, the residual difference of opinion was very small, focusing mainly on the likely positioning of Pelopidas if she had reduced speed prior to the collision.

The case was heard in the Queen's Bench Division (Admiralty Court) by Steel J. The judge had concerns as to certain features of the expert evidence.

The first point which Steel J. made was that, without leave of the court, expert evidence on matters of seamanship was not admissible. This was because:

"In admiralty practice [assessors] are not only technical advisers: they are sources of evidence as to the facts. In questions of nautical science and skill, relating to the management and movement of ships, a court, assisted by nautical assessors, obtains the information from them, not from sworn witnesses called by the parties." (*per* Lord Sumner in *The Owners of SS Australia v. The Owners of Cargo ex-Nautilis* [1927] A.C. 145).

Steel J. commented that his particular court had had the great advantage of assistance from the Elder Brethren of Trinity House in the role of assessors for a very long time. He considered that "the system has worked well, both from the perspective of the court in receiving sound and independent advice and from the perspective of the parties in saving costs. This court will strive to maintain the system, confident that it reflects best practice under CPR". Steel J. commented that if the parties wished to obtain nautical advice it was a matter for them, but that without an order of the court, the costs of obtaining such advice would not be recoverable.

Steel J. also commented on the use of illustrative plotting of tracks of vessels leading up to the collision, which now had become computerised. Various programmes existed which enabled much more accurate reconstructions to be made, influenced by a vast range of parameters. Steel J. remarked that this resulted in parties furnishing computerised plots prepared by experts, accompanied by a substantial amount of explanatory material. The judge, however, was of the view that it had led to the presentation of material which fell foul of the bar against admission of seamanship evidence. In addition, it led to the duplication, if not waste, of costs.

Steel J. encouraged the use of a selected brand of software, perhaps by a single expert, who would be able to furnish the parties (and the court) with reconstructions based on their favoured assumptions. Steel J. also re-emphasised the importance of keeping the role of plotting in perspective. Whilst margins of error were no doubt more limited than previously, they could not be eliminated. Steel J. was anxious to stress that a tiny margin of error could become highly significant. Reconstructions enabled the court and the parties to have a broad bird's eye view of events leading up to the collision. However, their true value was that:

11.072

> "They may sometimes enable the court to determine, not what may have happened, but what could not possibly have happened".

Steel J. considered it important for the parties to understand that

> "where a plot is to be relied upon to demonstrate what the tracks of the vessel must have been . . . the impact of the plotting is more effective if, despite assuming every margin of error in favour of a particular hypothesis, that outcome can be demonstrated to be highly improbable if not impossible".

The last point which Steel J. made on expert evidence was that whilst it was obviously desirable that margins of error be reduced as much as practicable, a sense of proportion must be maintained:

> "It is important that a degree of discipline is maintained as regards expert evidence where the resolution of the difference of opinion between the experts cannot have any material influence on the outcome of the action, it is incumbent on the parties to avoid incurring the costs of trying to achieve that resolution".

11.073

Comment: This is a good example of the courts stressing that expert evidence must be kept proportionate and in perspective. It also provides useful guidance as to how to use reconstructions and warns of the dangers of adducing "seamanship" evidence for which costs will not be recoverable.

VALUATION

Bandegani v. Norwich Union Fire Insurance Society Ltd (May 20, 1999) New Law 299058506

11.074   This case before the Court of Appeal (Henry L.J. and Holman J.) involved a small claim in which there was an issue as to the necessity of adducing expert evidence. Although the CPR did not apply directly to this case, its interest lies in the commentary of the judges as to how it would have been approached under the CPR.

This case related to an insurance claim as a result of damage to a car which had been bought for £1,500. The main point in dispute was the pre-accident value of the car. The claimant was claiming that the value of the car was the price he had paid for it (*i.e.* £1,500).

Neither side provided an expert report on this subject before the hearing. However, on the morning of the hearing, the defendant arrived at court with an expert witness and tendered a report by this expert. His view was that the book value of the car before the accident was £900. The claimant objected to the defendant relying on either the report or any oral evidence of the expert witness as he had not had any prior notice. He also requested an adjournment to enable him to obtain and adduce his own expert evidence as to the value.

11.075   The judge decided to disregard the evidence of the expert witness produced by the defendant and refused the claimant's application to adduce his own expert evidence as to value. In addition, he found that the claimant had failed to prove the value of the car, as in his evidence he had simply said that he had bought the car privately for £1,500. A distinction was drawn in this context between the price that the claimant had paid for the car and its actual market value, on the basis that the price paid did not afford any evidence as to value. The claimant applied to set aside the award.

The Court of Appeal found that the judge had misdirected himself in finding that the claimant's evidence as to what he had paid for the car did not and could not amount to evidence as to its value. The Court of Appeal was of the view that the price that someone had recently paid for a second-hand item may not be very strong evidence of its value and may be displaced by other reliable evidence that the true market value is different. However, it could not be said that this kind of evidence did not amount to any evidence of value:

> "As a matter of common sense, if the issue is as to the market value of an item and the item is widely available, such as a Nissan Cherry car, and it has just been traded at arm's length on the open market, then the price at which it was traded must have formed some evidence as to value, even if rebuttable."

The Court of Appeal made particular reference to the CPR. Indeed, Henry L.J. found that the case was originally conducted on the assumption that the question of the valuation of the car was a proper matter for the calling, in person, of expert evidence on both sides. Henry L.J. questioned that assumption on the grounds of proportionality. CPR r.27.5 provided in relation to the small claims track that "no expert may give evidence, whether written or oral, at a hearing without the permission of the court." Henry L.J. was of the view that the granting of such permission in cases like the case at hand should not be encouraged for reasons of proportionality. The evidence which could be used in such cases could instead be "published guides available in newsagents and used in the trade that give some indication as to the market price of second-hand cars which judges may find helpful". The view of Henry L.J. was that in ordinary cases such guides would give better evidential value for money than the calling of two experts to give oral evidence.

Comment: This case reminds us of the importance of proportionality   **11.076**
when deciding whether to call expert evidence and that in some cases other forms of evidence will be more appropriate.

North Holdings Ltd v. Southern Tropics Ltd [1999] 2 B.C.L.C. 625

This case before the Court of Appeal (Morritt and Aldous L.JJ.) related to a   **11.077**
request by a shareholder for valuation of shares. The relevance as to expert evidence rested in an *obiter* comment made by Aldous LJ.

Aldous L.J. stated that the approach to be adopted under the new CPR was set out in CPR r.1.4(2). There was a need for active case management at an early stage so as to reduce the time and expense involved in ascertaining the fair price for shares. Ample use should be made of the power to require a joint expert or the appointment of an assessor. It was to be anticipated that this would result in a substantial reduction in the number of applications to strike-out as the parties would realise that in most cases the court-imposed directions would result in a procedure which would be sufficiently quick and cheap as to make it unwise to insert a legal step, which might not succeed, and which, even if it did, would not save much expense.

Comment: This is an interesting indication from the Court of Appeal   **11.078**
that the overriding objective of the CPR will be applied particularly aggressively to valuations of shares.

UCB Corporate Services (formerly UCB Bank Plc) v. Halifax (SW) Ltd (in liquidation) (2000) 16 E.G. 137

This case before the Court of Appeal (Roch, Ward and Gage L.JJ.) related to   **11.079**
expert evidence on the valuation of property.

The matter arose in the context of a claim by UCB Corporate Services Ltd ("UCB") against surveyors for an alleged negligent valuation of property for mortgage purposes.

UCB's expert witness, a surveyor, was of the view that the development in question was a new small industrial unit located in a strong inner suburban town close to Central London. It was the sort of location which was likely to be in high demand in normal market conditions. However, his view was that, in April 1990, units had been available for sale and occupation for over six months and only five of the units constructed had been purchased or were subject to offers. He considered that this demonstrated a very slow rate of take-up for such development and that as a result 10 per cent had to be deducted from the open market valuation.

In contrast, the defendant's expert surveyor was of the view that "it would not have been appropriate to have suggested a discount in value". He said that he came to this view having considered the market conditions at the time, the fact that this was a new development and that the unit in question was "the most attractive and prominent part of the development".

11.080   In summary, UCB's expert considered that there was a blight in the market at that point and that the sale would in effect be a forced sale and would therefore be unlikely to sell at full value. On the other hand the defendant's surveyor was of the view that there was a lull in the market in the period before and after Christmas and that the value could expect a post-Christmas fresh impetus.

The judge preferred the defendant's expert's opinion:

> "I accept Mr Honeywill's views that as at April 1990 the demand for small business units, particularly if they were as attractive as these and in a good position in Kingston, could be expected to hold up. I therefore accept his view that it was a perfectly reasonable decision for Mr Ralph to make no discount for the 90-day clause . . . He was justified in reasoning that six units had been sold or were under offer in some six or seven months since completion of the development. In view of the demand for these attractive units in an attractive development, it was appropriate to make no discount for a 90-day sale."

The judge's finding was that the valuation was not negligent. On that basis, the claim failed.

The grounds of appeal were the judge's acceptance of the evidence of the defendant's expert. The claimant said it was plainly wrong because the external admitted factors drove one inexorably to the contrary conclusion. The facts contradicted the optimism expressed by the defendant's expert. If there was a lull before and after Christmas, then one would have expected the lull to have ended by about the end of January and would have expected that between the end of January and the end of April all of the remaining ten properties or most of the properties would have been sold, when the evidence was only that two had been sold and two were under offer.

The Court of Appeal found that on the basis that there was opinion evidence of experts at the trial, these opinions were either to be accepted or rejected by the judge. It was clearly within his permitted remit to accept the defendant's expert's view. The question which remained was whether the judge had evidence before him which justified his conclusion. Clearly in this case he did. On that basis UCB's appeal was dismissed.

11.081   **Comment:**   The appellant's case was essentially that common sense dictated that any valuation of a property on the basis of a 90-day sale as a mortgagee in possession must be calculated at a discount to the open market. This was an almost irrebuttable presumption. The Court of Appeal found that this was an attractive argument. However, it was clear that there could be circumstances where the market was so buoyant that one could conceive that the 90-day sale value would be the same as the open market value. On that basis, the question of the correct valuation came down to a question of fact which the judge had to decide on, having considered all of the evidence including the expert evidence. The Court of Appeal stressed that it would only be on rare occasions that an appellate court would interfere with the trial judge's finding of fact even when dealing with expert evidence.

Ferngold Plant Hire Ltd v. R Wenham (T/A BW Contractors) (March 13, 2000) unreported

This case before the Court of Appeal (Ward and Sedley L.JJ.) dealt with expert evidence as to valuation of specialist machinery. **11.082**

The claim was for damages for the loss of use of a Vermeer T600 highway trenching machine.

Valuation evidence was called by experts on each side. A Mr Cladeck gave evidence for the claimant. He had considerable experience of trenching machines. It was Mr Cladeck who had sold the machine in the first place. Mr Cladeck had looked for a replacement machine for the claimant and gave evidence that a machine became available in Germany in 1996. It was worth about £10,000 but the cost of reconditioning it would have brought that cost up to £69,000. In his report, Mr Cladeck also provided figures for his commission and a sum in respect of a warranty. His total figure came to £87,000. One machine had also been sold by him for £138,000.

A Mr Daniel was called for the defendants. He was a director of a contracting company, with long experience in the procurement, maintenance and disposal of all plant, including trenchers of this kind. Mr Daniel gave evidence that he had seen a comparable machine sell at auction three years earlier for £21,000. He also provided evidence as to auction prices of comparable machines.

The judge's task was: "to choose between the expert evidence of [the] two valuers as to the value of the machine at the time of its loss". The question for the judge was to consider which he preferred:

> "The claimant's valuer gave evidence of the value of one real machine, which he saw and knew before he offered it for sale at £138,000 and the notional value of the German machine, which he had also inspected. The defendant's expert relied on the notional value, if improved, of the machine he saw sold some three years previously in Bristol."

The judge allowed £87,000 as the capital value of that machine and a further £15,000 for the three years of loss of use of the profit to be derived from the use of that machine. To that he added interest.

On appeal, the Court of Appeal commented that the judge was making a finding of fact. It recognised that it was the loss to the claimant which was the material consideration. What it was worth to the claimant could only be assessed by considering the cost to the claimant of replacing it. The test was, therefore, not simply an auction value but the value of the machine to the loser.

The Court of Appeal found that against that background:

"The judge's approach . . . amounts quite clearly to no more than preferring the claimant's specialist and explaining why he did so, which was partly because of the importance of a history which gave the machine more commercial credibility than a pig in a poke bought at auction. It was a reasonable requirement of the claimant to have the confidence in the machine which it had in the old".

It was in addition acceptable for the judge to take the view that to spend £138,000 would not have been a reasonable act and that the proper approach, therefore, was to shop around and establish a value that the machine would command.

11.083   **Comment:**   The interest of this case lies in the guidance as to how the courts will approach valuation of specialist machinery. It demonstrates that the courts will take into account the specific concerns and requirements of a party when selecting a replacement machine.

WILLS

Wilkes v. Wilkes (June 8, 2000) unreported

11.084   In this case, Mr Terence Etherton Q.C., in the Chancery Division, dismissed a claim for revocation of probate of a will. Before holding that the testatrix was of testamentary capacity, he heard conflicting expert and factual evidence.

The claimant called as his expert a Dr Whale, a consultant physician at Herts and Essex Hospital. He specialised in the care of the elderly and had been a consultant since 1982. However, he had never met the testatrix, and his expert evidence was given by reference to her medical records. Dr Whale's conclusion that the testatrix was probably incapable of making her will rested on three principal matters: first, the evidence of widespread brain damage; second, the fact that the testatrix had Parkinson's disease; and third, the testatrix's auditory impairment and extreme age. Nevertheless, the judge found Dr Whale's evidence to be measured, objective and very helpful.

The judge concluded that although he placed great weight on the evidence of the expert witness, he could not ignore the considerable body of evidence given by independent factual witnesses as to their dealings with the testatrix. He was influenced by the fact that three of the witnesses were in frequent contact with the testatrix over substantial periods prior to her death. Although all of these witnesses had become friends of the defendant, the judge said that he had no reason to doubt their integrity or honesty.

The judge concluded, taking the evidence as a whole, that the defendant had discharged the burden of establishing that the testatrix had testamentary capacity at the date of giving instructions for and executing her will.

11.085   **Comment:**   This case is interesting for the fact that although the judge placed great weight on the views of the expert evidence, in the end he ultimately came to a different conclusion to that of the expert witness, even though there was no other expert evidence.

This case (and *Fuller v. Strum* — see below) sits uncomfortably with the Court of Appeal decision in *In Re B (child)* [2000] 1 W.L.R. 790. In this case the

Court of Appeal stated that evidence from factual witnesses will only rarely be preferred over logically analysed expert medical evidence. In *In Re B (child)*, there was uncontroverted evidence from various medical experts regarding the timing of injuries to a baby. However, the first instance judge also heard evidence from the grandmother of the baby and from a family friend. This evidence was difficult to reconcile with the evidence of the experts. The judge preferred the factual evidence, but on appeal the Court of Appeal held that the judge was not entitled to do so because he did not have evidence before him that made the "uncontroverted medical evidence logically insupportable". The Court of Appeal was of the view that "the credibility or otherwise of the lay witnesses on the facts of this case . . . cannot stand so high as to make the evidence of the two consultant radiologists of no effect".

Fuller v. Strum, The Times, February 14, 2001

This case, in the Chancery Division, provides an interesting example of a case   11.086
where a judge prefers the evidence of a witness of fact to the evidence of an expert witness, notwithstanding the fact that the issue is expert evidence.

The facts of the case can be simply stated. Before he died, Max Strum diverted about half of his estate away from his next of kin (the defendant) in favour of the claimant. Mr Strum's son claimed that the will was forged.

Each side had consulted a handwriting expert, and each expert had come up with a different answer. In the end, the master ordered a single joint expert to be appointed — a Dr Audrey Giles, the well-known handwriting expert from the Giles Document Laboratory. The reports of the other experts were not admitted as evidence. Dr Giles produced a comparison chart containing acknowledged and genuine signatures of Mr Strum as well as the questioned signature on the disputed will. Dr Giles' evidence was that the number and nature of the differences between the signature on the will and the genuine signatures led her to conclude that there was, in her words, "very strong positive evidence" that the signature on the will was a forgery.

Importantly, Dr Giles did not give evidence orally. The judge was told that this was in the interest of saving costs. However, he said that "in a case where the factual evidence is in conflict with the expert's conclusion, the judge is faced with a dilemma, and it would have assisted me greatly to have had the opportunity to put this dilemma to Dr Giles, and to have obtained as much assistance as I could from her evidence". The judge added that, while the dispassionate opinion of a court-appointed expert would have been of great assistance, had she been called to give oral evidence, he thought that in the absence of such oral evidence, examination and cross-examination of the original two experts would have assisted him more.

The judge concluded that in relation to this type of expert evidence, the judge is entitled to form his own view, having regard to, and balancing, the other evidence available to him in the case (the judge had listened to several witnesses of fact). The judge found that the central reasoning as to why Dr Giles found that the will was forged was the number and nature of the differences between the signature on the will and the genuine signatures of Mr Strum. In that respect, her evidence fell outside the purely scientific category in respect of which the judge would be helpless without expert assistance. In conclusion, the judge held that he was free to decide the forgery issue for himself, and held that Mr Strum did indeed sign the will, albeit with a signature that varied somewhat from his usual signature.

11.087   **Comment:**   This is another example of a first instance decision where the judge came to a different conclusion to that of the expert witness. Again, this decision was made despite the Court of Appeal decision in *In Re B (child)* [2000] 1 W.L.R. 790 where it was held that if the expert evidence is logically supportable, a judge will need a very good reason for preferring the evidence of a factual witness.

This case is also interesting in view of the fact that the judge said that he would have found the expert witnesses instructed by the parties of more use than the non-oral evidence of the court-appointed single joint expert. This is a warning to parties to balance carefully the desire to save costs against the effective presentation of expert evidence. In this case, the failure to properly present the expert evidence invited the judge to come to a view contrary to that of the expert witness.

CHAPTER 12
Written questions to experts

CPR r.35.6 provides that a party may put to the other side's expert or a single **12.001**
joint expert written questions about his report. This is intended to facilitate
the exchange of information between the parties prior to trial. The provision
is given teeth by virtue of CPR r.35.6(4), which provides that if the expert does
not answer any question the court may order that the evidence cannot be
relied upon. The provision is innovative and should reduce the need for cross-
examination at trial because it can be done without the court's involvement
and prior to trial. Certainly, the two Court of Appeal cases reported below
demonstrate that the courts are enthusiastically taking up the spirit of CPR
r.35.6.

Two interesting questions on this subject which have not yet been considered
by the courts are the excessive use of questions by parties and an expert's failure to respond.

In relation to the first issue, the White Book Service "Civil Procedure" notes
that an approach to dealing with excessive or onerous questions is for the expert
to ask the court for directions. It is expected that the number and content of
questions will be judged according to the principle of proportionality. This issue
is sure to arise in case law in the near future.

As to the second issue, CPR r.35.6(4) fails to make provision for a time within
which a response must be given to a written question. The first case to deal with
this issue may prompt an amendment to the rules on this issue. In the meantime,
the notes to CPR r.35.6 in the White Book Service "Civil Procedure" state that
"in most circumstances 28 days would be reasonable". The Vice-Chancellor's
Working Party draft Code of Guidance on Expert Evidence recommends the
same response time.

Nicholson v. Halton General Hospital (NHS Trust) [1999] P.I.Q.R. P310

This case before the Court of Appeal (Beldam L.J. and Sumner J.) was specif- **12.002**
ically concerned with the question of whether one expert can interview the
other expert before the trial of the action, or whether any inquiry should be
restricted to written requests.

The claimant had been employed since 1987 by the defendant Hospital Trust.
She used ultrasonic equipment which involved extensive use of her right arm. It
was common ground that the claimant had radial tunnel syndrome. The issues
between the parties were causation and, if causation was established, whether it
arose due to the negligence of the defendants.

The claimant underwent remedial surgery carried out by a Professor Stanley.
The claimant disclosed Professor Stanley's operating notes to the defendants. The defendants instructed Mr Spigelman, an orthopaedic surgeon. Mr
Spigelman accepted the diagnosis that had been made, but he disputed the question of what could or did cause that condition. He therefore wanted to contact

Professor Stanley to ask him what anatomical reason was found at operation. The claimant refused to allow Mr Spigelman to speak to Professor Stanley.

The Court of Appeal held that the only restriction a claimant in these circumstances could reasonably seek would be that the information be confined to that which is relevant to the issues then existing between the parties. Accordingly, once that is decided, "the question of how a defendant obtains the information must . . . be one for the defendant. Unless there is some good reason, it is not for the claimant to impose any conditions other than to ensure that the information sought is relevant to the issue existing between the parties".

The judgment also dealt with the conflict which arose for Professor Stanley between a request from the court for information and his duty of confidentiality arising out of his patient-to-doctor relationship. The court found that in the circumstances of this case, it could stay the claim until the claimant consented to waiving his right of confidentiality.

12.003   **Comment:**   The interest of this case lies in showing that, when collecting information, an expert is free in his choice of how to obtain this information and that this can include obtaining information orally. It will be interesting to see whether subsequent courts take the same approach after the Vice-Chancellor's Working Party draft Code of Guidance on Expert Evidence is finalised. This contains guidance on meetings between experts and states that the parties, the lawyers and the experts should co-operate to produce concise agendas for any discussion between experts.

Mutch v. Allen, The Independent, March 5, 2001

12.004   This personal injury case in the Court of Appeal (Simon Brown and Longmore L.JJ.) has produced useful judicial clarification on the use of written questions to experts.

CPR r.35.6(1) provides that: "a party may put to (a) an expert instructed by another party; or (b) a single joint expert appointed under r.35.7, written questions about his report".

The claimant was seriously injured in a road traffic accident while travelling as a backseat passenger in a car driven by the defendant. General damages apart, the claimant's special damage and future loss were particularised at over £500,000. The claimant was not, however, wearing a seat belt, and the defendant alleged contributory negligence.

The claimant's principal report was prepared by a Professor Solomon. It noted that the claimant was not wearing a seat belt at the time of the accident, but it said nothing as to the consequences of that failure. The defendant's solicitors wrote to Professor Solomon asking him to clarify his report under the provisions of CPR r.35.6 in these terms:

> "we should be grateful if you could confirm whether the severity of Mr Mutch's orthopaedic injuries would have been reduced materially, if not prevented altogether, had he been wearing a seat belt. If the answer to this question is positive, we should be grateful if you would indicate which injuries would have been avoided altogether by the use of a seat belt and which injuries would still have been sustained but would have been less severe."

The letter was copied to the claimant's solicitors who objected to the ques-   **12.005**
tions and instructed Professor Solomon not to reply.

At a case management conference a District Judge allowed an application by
the defendant to put the questions to the claimant's medical expert. To assist the
expert, the claimant's solicitors sent the expert further information, and, on the
basis of this information, the expert provided answers in a letter which severely
damaged the claimant's case. In essence, it confirmed that the injuries which the
claimant suffered would have been much less severe had he been fully restrained
by an effective seat belt.

At a pre-trial review, Judge Hutton ordered that the expert's answers in the
letter should not be admitted at trial.

However, on appeal to the Court of Appeal, the court held that the expert's
answers should have been admitted in evidence. The court said that the first
point to note was that irrespective of whether or not the questions were strictly
"for the purpose only of clarification", the court had given permission to put
them to the expert. Further, the claimant had helped administer them without
objection.

Moreover, the Court of Appeal noted that the footnote to CPR r.35.6(1) in
the White Book Service "Civil Procedure" envisaged not only clarification of a
report, but extension as well. The footnote states: "in a given case, were it not
possible to achieve such clarification or extension of a report, the court, for that
reason alone, may feel obliged to direct that the expert witness should testify at
trial". (Although not noted in the judgment to this case, the footnote does also
state that clarification should not be used to require the expert to expand significantly on his report.) The Court of Appeal noted that had Professor
Solomon simply been called to give evidence, the defendant could have asked
him exactly the same questions in cross-examination.

The court then said that the effect of the claimant's failure to wear a seat belt
on the severity of his injuries was a matter upon which expert medical evidence
would be of the greatest materiality to the case.

Finally, as highlighted by the Court of Appeal: "the most fundamental difficulty with the judge's approach however is that it overlooks the essential reform
sought to be achieved by Part 35". The court said that the CPR was a new
regime designed to ensure that experts no longer serve the exclusive interest of
those by whom they were retained, but instead contribute to a just resolution of
the dispute.

Comment: In this case, the main reason why the Court of Appeal ruled   **12.006**
that the expert's letter should be admissible seems to be the fact that the court
had given permission for the questions to be put to the expert. The Court of
Appeal was also influenced by the fact that the expert evidence was "of the
greatest materiality". Other cases may arise where a party simply complies with
a request for answers about an expert report under CPR r.35.6(1), without the
necessity of obtaining a court order. In other cases the expert evidence may also
be of less importance. However, it would seem that the final reason of the Court
of Appeal, the essential reform sought to be achieved by Part 35, will always
prevent one party from seeking to argue that the answers provided in accordance with CPR r.35.6(1) should be inadmissible. Simon Brown's L.J. words are
a telling reminder in this respect:

"Had Professor Solomon ultimately expressed an opinion more favourable to the claimant as to the likely causative effect of not wearing a seat belt, it can hardly be doubted that he would have enthusiastically adopted it as part of his case. The question arises, having in the event been disappointed [with] the Professor's answer, could the claimant then properly have it annulled on the footing that, as the judge put it, 'the claimant does not have to prove the defendant's case'. The defendant understandably submits not."

With this the Court of Appeal agreed.

Appendix 1
Part 1 of the CPR
Overriding objective

Contents of this Part App 1.001

The Overriding Objective

1.1 (1) These Rules are a new procedural code with the overriding objective of enabling the court to deal with cases justly.

   (2) Dealing with a case justly includes, so far as is practicable —
      (a) ensuring that the parties are on an equal footing;
      (b) saving expense;
      (c) dealing with the case in ways which are proportionate —
         (i)   to the amount of money involved;
         (ii) to the importance of the case;
         (iii) to the complexity of the issues; and
         (iv) to the financial position of each party;
      (d) ensuring that it is dealt with expeditiously and fairly; and
      (e) allotting to it an appropriate share of the court's resources, while taking into account the need to allot resources to other cases.

Application by the Court of the Overriding Objective App 1.002

1.2 The court must seek to give effect to the overriding objective when it —

   (a) exercises any power given to it by the Rules; or
   (b) interprets any rule.

Duty of the Parties

1.3 The parties are required to help the court to further the overriding objective.

Court's Duty to Manage Cases App 1.003

1.4 (1) The court must further the overriding objective by actively managing cases.

   (2) Active case management includes –
      (a) encouraging the parties to co-operate with each other in the conduct of the proceedings;
      (b) identifying the issues at an early stage;
      (c) deciding promptly which issues need full investigation and trial and accordingly disposing summarily of the others;
      (d) deciding the order in which issues are to be resolved;
      (e) encouraging the parties to use an alternative dispute resolution (GL) procedure if the court considers that appropriate and facilitating the use of such procedure;
      (f) helping the parties to settle the whole or part of the case;
      (g) fixing timetables or otherwise controlling the progress of the case;
      (h) considering whether the likely benefits of taking a particular step justify the cost of taking it;

      (i) dealing with as many aspects of the case as it can on the same occasion;

      (j) dealing with the case without the parties needing to attend at court;

      (k) making use of technology; and

      (l) giving directions to ensure that the trial of a case proceeds quickly and efficiently.

Appendix 2
Part 35 of the CPR
Experts and Assessors

Contents of this Part

App 2.001

Duty to Restrict Expert Evidence

App 2.002

35.1 Expert evidence shall be restricted to that which is reasonably required to resolve the proceedings.

Interpretation

App 2.003

35.2 A reference to an "expert" in this Part is a reference to an expert who has been instructed to give or prepare evidence for the purpose of court proceedings.

Experts — Overriding Duty to the Court

App 2.004

35.3 (1) It is the duty of an expert to help the court on the matters within his expertise.

(2) This duty overrides any obligation to the person from whom he has received instructions or by whom he is paid.

Court's Power to Restrict Expert Evidence

App 2.005

35.4 (1) No party may call an expert or put in evidence an expert's report without the court's permission.

(2) When a party applies for permission under this rule he must identify —
   (a) the field in which he wishes to rely on expert evidence; and
   (b) where practicable the expert in that field on whose evidence he wishes to rely.

(3) If permission is granted under this rule it shall be in relation only to the expert named or the field identified under paragraph (2).

(4) The court may limit the amount of the expert's fees and expenses that the party who wishes to rely on the expert may recover from any other party.

General Requirement for Expert Evidence to be Given in a Written Report

App 2.006

35.5 (1) Expert evidence is to be given in a written report unless the court directs otherwise.

(2) If a claim is on the fast track, the court will not direct an expert to attend a hearing unless it is necessary to do so in the interests of justice.

App 2.007   **Written Questions to Experts**

35.6 (1) A party may put to —
(a) an expert instructed by another party; or
(b) a single joint expert appointed under rule 35.7,
written questions about his report.

(2) Written questions under paragraph (1) —
(a) may be put once only;
(b) must be put within 28 days of service of the expert's report; and
(c) must be for the purpose only of clarification of the report,
unless in any case —
(i) the court gives permission; or
(ii) the other party agrees.

(3) An expert's answers to questions put in accordance with paragraph (1) shall be treated as part of the expert's report.

(4) Where —
(a) a party has put a written question to an expert instructed by another party in accordance with this rule; and
(b) the expert does not answer that question,
the court may make one or both of the following orders in relation to the party who instructed the expert —
(i) that the party may not rely on the evidence of that expert; or
(ii) that the party may not recover the fees and expenses of that expert from any other party.

App 2.008   **Court's Power to Direct that Evidence is to be Given by a Single Joint Expert**

35.7 (1) Where two or more parties wish to submit expert evidence on a particular issue, the court may direct that the evidence on that issue is to given by one expert only.

(2) The parties wishing to submit the expert evidence are called "the instructing parties".

(3) Where the instructing parties cannot agree who should be the expert, the court may —
(a) select the expert from a list prepared or identified by the instructing parties; or
(b) direct that the expert be selected in such other manner as the court may direct.

App 2.009   **Instructions to a Single Joint Expert**

35.8 (1) Where the court gives a direction under rule 35.7 for a single joint expert to be used, each instructing party may give instructions to the expert.

(2) When an instructing party gives instructions to the expert he must, at the same time, send a copy of the instructions to the other instructing parties.

(3) The court may give directions about —
(a) the payment of the expert's fees and expenses; and
(b) any inspection, examination or experiments which the expert wishes to carry out.

(4) The court may, before an expert is instructed —
(a) limit the amount that can be paid by way of fees and expenses to the expert; and
(b) direct that the instructing parties pay that amount into court.

(5) Unless the court otherwise directs, the instructing parties are jointly and severally liable$^{(GL)}$ for the payment of the expert's fees and expenses.

Power of Court to Direct a Party to Provide Information App 2.010

35.9   Where a party has access to information which is not reasonably available to the other party, the court may direct the party who has access to the information to —
   (a) prepare and file a document recording the information; and
   (b) serve a copy of that document on the other party.

Contents of Report App 2.011

35.10 (1) An expert's report must comply with the requirements set out in the relevant practice direction.

(2) At the end of an expert's report there must be a statement that —
   (a) the expert understands his duty to the court; and
   (b) he has complied with that duty.

(3) The expert's report must state the substance of all material instructions, whether written or oral, on the basis of which the report was written.

(4) The instructions referred to in paragraph (3) shall not be privileged against disclosure but the court will not, in relation to those instructions —
   (a) order disclosure of any specific document; or
   (b) permit any questioning in court, other than by the party who instructed the expert,
   unless it is satisfied that there are reasonable grounds to consider the statement of instructions given under paragraph (3) to be inaccurate or incomplete.

Use by One Party of Expert's Report Disclosed by Another App 2.012

35.11 Where a party has disclosed an expert's report, any party may use that expert's report as evidence at the trial.

Discussions Between Experts App 2.013

35.12 (1) The court may, at any stage, direct a discussion between experts for the purpose of requiring the experts to —
   (a) identify the issues in the proceedings; and
   (b) where possible, reach agreement on an issue.

(2) The court may specify the issues which the experts must discuss.

(3) The court may direct that following a discussion between the experts they must prepare a statement for the court showing —
   (a) those issues on which they agree; and
   (b) those issues on which they disagree and a summary of their reasons for disagreeing.
(4) The content of the discussion between the experts shall not be referred to at the trial unless the parties agree.

(5) Where experts reach agreement on an issue during their discussions, the agreement shall not bind the parties unless the parties expressly agree to be bound by the agreement.

Consequence of Failure to Disclose Expert's Report App 2.014

35.13 A party who fails to disclose an expert's report may not use the report at the trial or call the expert to give evidence orally unless the court gives permission.

Expert's Right to Ask Court for Directions App 2.015

35.14 (1) An expert may file a written request for directions to assist him in carrying out his function as an expert.

(2) An expert may request directions under paragraph (1) without giving notice to any party.

(3) The court, when it gives directions, may also direct that a party be served with —
(a) a copy of the directions; and
(b) a copy of the request for directions.

App 2.016   **Assessors**

35.15 (1) This rule applies where the court appoints one or more persons (an "assessor") under section 70 of the Supreme Court Act 1981[1] or section 63 of the County Courts Act 1984[2].

(2) The assessor shall assist the court in dealing with a matter in which the assessor has skill and experience.

(3) An assessor shall take such part in the proceedings as the court may direct and in particular the court may —
(a) direct the assessor to prepare a report for the court on any matter at issue in the proceedings; and
(b) direct the assessor to attend the whole or any part of the trial to advise the court on any such matter.

(4) If the assessor prepares a report for the court before the trial has begun —
(a) the court will send a copy to each of the parties; and
(b) the parties may use it at trial.

(5) The remuneration to be paid to the assessor for his services shall be determined by the court and shall form part of the costs of the proceedings.

(6) The court may order any party to deposit in the court office a specified sum in respect of the assessor's fees and, where it does so, the assessor will not be asked to act until the sum has been deposited.

(7) Paragraphs (5) and (6) do not apply where the remuneration of the assessor is to be paid out of money provided by Parliament.

---

[1] 1981 c.54.
[2] 1984 c.28. Section 63 was amended by S.I. 1998/2940.

Appendix 3
Practice Direction — Experts
and Assessors

Part 35 is intended to limit the use of oral expert evidence to that which is reasonably required. In addition, where possible, matters requiring expert evidence should be dealt with by a single expert. Permission of the court is always required either to call an expert or to put an expert's report in evidence.

Form and Content of Expert's Reports   App 3.002

1.1 An expert's report should be addressed to the court and not to the party from whom the expert has received his instructions.

1.2 An expert's report must:

    (1) give details of the expert's qualifications,

    (2) give details of any literature or other material which the expert has relied on in making the report,

    (3) say who carried out any test or experiment which the expert has used for the report and whether or not the test or experiment has been carried out under the expert's supervision,

    (4) give the qualifications of the person who carried out any such test or experiment, and

    (5) where there is a range of opinion on the matters dealt with in the report —
        (i) summarise the range of opinion, and
        (ii) give reasons for his own opinion,

    (6) contain a summary of the conclusions reached,

    (7) contain a statement that the expert understands his duty to the court and has complied with that duty (rule 35.10(2)), and

    (8) contain a statement setting out the substance of all material instructions (whether written or oral). The statement should summarise the facts and instructions given to the expert which are material to the opinions expressed in the report or upon which those opinions are based (rule 35.10(3)).

1.3 An expert's report must be verified by a statement of truth as well as containing the statements required in paragraph 1.2 (7) and (8) above.

1.4 The form of the statement of truth is as follows:

' I believe that the facts I have stated in this report are true and that the opinions I have expressed are correct.'

1.5 Attention is drawn to rule 32.14 which sets out the consequences of verifying a document containing a false statement without an honest belief in its truth.

(For information about statements of truth see Part 22 and the practice direction which supplements it.)

1.6 In addition, an expert's report should comply with the requirements of any approved expert's protocol.

App 3.003   **Information**

2   Under Rule 35.9 the court may direct a party with access to information which is not reasonably available to another party to serve on that other party a document which records the information. The document served must include sufficient details of all the facts, tests, experiments and assumptions which underlie any part of the information to enable the party on whom it is served to make, or to obtain, a proper interpretation of the information and an assessment of its significance.

Instructions

App 3.004   3   The instructions referred to in paragraph 1.2(8) will not be protected by privilege (see rule 35.10(4)). But cross-examination of the expert on the contents of his instructions will not be allowed unless the court permits it (or unless the party who gave the instructions consents to it). Before it gives permission the court must be satisfied that there are reasonable grounds to consider that the statement in the report of the substance of the instructions is inaccurate or incomplete. If the court is so satisfied, it will allow the cross-examination where it appears to be in the interests of justice to do so.

Questions to Experts

App 3.005   4.1   Questions asked for the purpose of clarifying the expert's report (see rule 35.6) should be put, in writing, to the expert not later than 28 days after receipt of the expert's report (see paragraphs 1.2 to 1.5 above as to verification).

4.2   Where a party sends a written question or questions direct to an expert and the other party is represented by solicitors, a copy of the questions should, at the same time, be sent to those solicitors.

4.3   The party or parties instructing the expert must pay any fees charged by that expert for answering questions put under rule 35.6. This does not affect any decision of the court as to the party who is ultimately to bear the expert's costs.

Single Expert

App 3.006   5   Where the court has directed that the evidence on a particular issue is to be given by one expert only (rule 35.7) but there are a number of disciplines relevant to that issue, a leading expert in the dominant discipline should be identified as the single expert. He should prepare the general part of the report and be responsible for annexing or incorporating the contents of any reports from experts in other disciplines.

App 3.007   **Assessors**

6.1   An assessor may be appointed to assist the court under rule 35.15. Not less than 21 days before making any such appointment, the court will notify each party in writing of the name of the proposed assessor, of the matter in respect of which the assistance of the assessor will be sought and of the qualifications of the assessor to give that assistance.

6.2   Where any person has been proposed for appointment as an assessor, objection to him, either personally or in respect of his qualification, may be taken by any party.

6.3   Any such objection must be made in writing and filed with the court within 7 days of receipt of the notification referred to in paragraph 6.1 and will be taken into account by the court in deciding whether or not to make the appointment (section 63(5) of the County Courts Act 1984).

6.4   Copies of any report prepared by the assessor will be sent to each of the parties but the assessor will not give oral evidence or be open to cross-examination or questioning.

Appendix 4
Extract from the Commercial
Court Guide
Evidence for Trial

H1 WITNESS OF FACT App 4.001

Preparation and Form of Witness Statements

H1.1 The pre-trial timetable will usually include directions for the service of witness statements.

H1.2 Witness statements must comply with the requirements xx the practice direction supplementing CPR Part 32. For the avoidance of doubt, all witness statements must be signed or initialled on each page, unless the Court otherwise orders.

H1.3 The following points are emphasised:

a. whilst it is recognised that in commercial cases, a witness statement will usually be prepared by legal representatives, the witness statement must, so far as practicable, be in the witness's own words;

b. the witness statement must indicate which of the statements made in it are made from the witness's own knowledge and which are matters of information and belief (giving the source for any matters of information and belief);

c. the witness statement must include a statement by the witness that he believes the matters in it are true; a witness statement is the equivalent of the oral evidence which that witness would, if called, give as his evidence in chief at the trial and proceedings for contempt of court may be brought against a person if he makes, or causes to be made, a false statement in a witness statement without an honest belief in its truth (see CPR 32.14(1));

d. a witness statement should not be longer than necessary and should not contain lengthy renditions of correspondence.

H1.4 The rules of any relevant professional body regarding the drafting of witness statements must also be observed.

Fluency of Witness App 4.002

H1.5 Where a witness is not sufficiently fluent in English to give his evidence in English, the witness statement should be in the witness's own language and a translation provided.

H1.6 Where a witness is not fluent in English but can make himself understood in broken English and can understand written English, provided that these matters are indicated in the witness statement the statement need not be in his own words. It must however be written so as to express as accurately as possible the substance of his evidence.

Witness Statement as Evidence in Chief App 4.003

H1.7 By CPR 32.5(3) where a witness is called to give oral evidence, his witness statement is to stand as his evidence in chief unless the Court orders otherwise. In an appropriate case the Trial Judge may require the whole or any part of the witness's evidence in chief to be given orally.

App 4.004   **Additional Evidence from a Witness**

H1.8   By CPR 32.5(3) a witness giving oral evidence at trial may with the permission of the Court amplify his witness statement and give evidence in relation to new matters which have arisen since the witness statement was served on the other parties. CPR 32.5(4) provides that this permission will be given only if the Court considers that there is good reason not to confine the evidence of the witness to the contents of his witness statement. In the Commercial Court a supplemental witness statement should normally be served where the witness proposes materially to add to, alter, correct or retract from what is in his original witness statement. Permission will be required for the service of a supplemental statement.

App 4.005   **Notice of Decision Not to Call a Witness**

H1.9   Where a party has decided not to call a witness whose witness statement has been served to give oral evidence at trial, prompt notice of this decision should be given to all other parties. The party should make plain when he gives this notice whether he proposes to put, or seek to put, the witness statement in as hearsay evidence. If he does not put the witness statement in as hearsay evidence, CPR 32.5(5) allows any other party to put it in as hearsay evidence.

App 4.006   **Witness Summonses**

H1.10   CPR 34.2 to 34.7 deal with witness summonses, including a summons for a witness to attend court or to produce documents in advance of the date fixed for trial. As for service (CPR 34.6), in the Commercial Court witness summonses are to be served by the parties, not the Court.

App 4.007   **H2 EXPERT WITNESSES**

Application for Permission

H2.1   Any application for permission to call an expert witness, or serve an expert's report, should normally be made at the Case Management Conference.

H2.2   CPR Part 35 applies to proceedings in the Commercial List subject to the exceptions and further provisions contained in this section of the Guide and in Appendix 12. The practice direction supplementing CPR Part 35 also applies, again subject to the exceptions and further provisions contained in this section of the Guide and in Appendix 12.

App 4.008   **Separate Experts**

H2.3   In the Commercial Court, as in cases generally, the parties should bear in mind that expert evidence can lead to unnecessary expenditure, and they should be prepared to consider the use of single joint experts. However, cases in the Commercial Court frequently are of a size and of a complexity or nature such that the use of single joint experts is not appropraite. In such cases, parties will generally be given permission each to call one expert whom they have retained in each field requiring expert evidence. In this Guide these experts are called "separate experts". On occasion there will be questions about appropriate fields of expertise, and the Court will have to resolve such questions.

App 4.009   **Single Joint Expert**

H2.4   CPR 35.7 permits the Court to direct that there be a single joint expert rather than separate experts. Such a direction may be made in the Commercial Court in an appropriate case. The complexity and value of the case are relevant here; some cases are more straightforward and of lower value than others. There is, however, no presumption in the Commercial Court in favour of single joint experts. And where in an appropriate case both parties wish to instruct separate experts a direction in favour of a single joint expert may possibly be infrequently made.

H2.5   In some cases the appointment of a single joint expert to carry out an examination at the very beginning of a case may be appropriate. But even here the Commercial Court recognises that the use of separate experts may bring greater advantage, not least in providing the facility for each party to take separate expert advice. However in such a case whenever possible joint inspections by both experts are to be encouraged.

H2.6   Ocasionally in a complex commercial case where a meeting of separate experts is likely to involve unusual difficulties or complexities the use of a single joint expert may be combined with the use of (separate) experts retained by the parties. Here the function of the single joint expert might be, not to report or give evidence, but to chair and facilitate meetings of separate experts.

H2.7   Paragraph 5 of the practice direction supplementing CPR Part 35 indicates that where the Court has directed that the evidence on a particular issue be given by one expert only but there are a number of disciplines relevant to that issue, a leading expert in the dominant discipline will prepare the general part of a report and will annex or incorporate the contents of any reports from experts in other disciplines. Use of this procedure may be infrequent in the Commercial Court. If reports from experts in a number xx disciplines or fields are necessary on a particular issue, the Court will require to be persuaded before allowing evidence to be given other than directly by each expert in each discipline or field.

H2.8   When the use of a single joint expert is contemplated, the Court will expect the parties to co-operate in developing, and agreeing to the greatest possible extent, terms of reference for that expert. In most cases the terms of reference will (in particular) detail what the expert is asked to do, identity any documentary materials he is asked to consider and specify any assumptions he is asked to make.

Requirements of General Application in Relation to Expert Evidence   App 4.010

H2.9   The requirements of Appendix 12 will apply in relation to all aspects of expert evidence (including expert reports, meetings of experts and expert evidence given orally) unless the Court orders otherwise. Legal representatives should ensure that Appendix 12 is at the earliest point drawn to the attention of an expert retained by a party.

Form and Content of Expert's Reports   App 4.011

H2.10 The requirements at paragraphs 1.1 and 1.2 of the practice direction supplementing CPR Part 35 should be followed. Paragraphs 1.3 and 1.4 of the practice direction are addressed at paragraphs H2.14 and H2.15 below.

H2.11 The expert should take care always to state clearly the questions or issues with which he is dealing in his report.

H2.12 In stating the substance of all material instructions on the basis of which his report is written (see CPR 35.10(3) and paragraph 1.2(8) of the practice direction supplementing CPR Part 35) an expert witness should state the facts or assumptions upon which his opinion is based. If any of the facts stated are within his own direct knowledge he should make clear which those are. If a stated assumption is, in the opinion of the expert witness, unreasonable or unlikely he should state that clearly.

H2.13 It is useful if a report contains a glossary of significant technical terms.

App 4.012   **Statement of Truth**

> H2.14 At the end of the expert's report there must be a statement that:
> a. the expert understands his duty to the Court and has complied with that duty (see CPR 35.10(2));
> b. the expert has read and understood Appendix 12 to the Commercial Court Guide;
> c. he has complied and will cintinue to comply with Appendix 12 at all stages of his involvement in the case;
> d. the assumptions upon which his opinion is based are not in his opinion unreasonable or unlikely assumptions (or, where in his opinion any assumption is unreasonable or unlikely, that is clearly stated);
> e. the facts stated in his report that are facts within his own direct knowledge have been identified as such and are true;
> f. the opinions expressed in his report represent his true professional opinion.
>
> The report must be signed by the expert.

> H2.15 In the Commercial Court the requirement for a statement in the terms indicated at paragraph H2.14 above takes the place of the requirement for a statement of truth in the terms provided xx paragraph 1.4 of the practice direction supplementing CPR Part 35 (and see paragraph 1.3 of the practice direction supplementing CPR Part 22). As with any document verified by a statement of truth, proceedings for contempt of court may be brought against a person if he makes, or causes to be made, without an honest belief in its truth, a false statement in an expert's report verified by a statement of truth (see paragraph 1.5 of the practice direction supplementing CPR Part 35).

App 4.013   **Request by an Expert to the Court for Directions**

> H2.16 An expert may file with the Court a written request for directions to assist him in carrying out his function as expert, but:
> a. at least 7 days before he does so (or such shorter period as the Court may direct) he should provide a copy of his proposed request to the party instructing him;
> b. at least 4 days before he does so (or such shorter period as the Court may direct) he should provide a copy of his proposed request to all other parties.

> H2.17 In the Commercial Court this procedure takes the place of CPR 35.14. It is intended to reduce the risk of an expert accidentally informing the Court about, or about matters connected with, communications or potential communications between the parties that are without prejudice or privileged. The expert may properly be privy to the content of these communications because he has been asked to assist the party instructing him to evaluate them. The procedure does not prevent the expert from filing a request for directions, but ensures that one or other party can approach the Court first if the request proposed by the expert would result in his informing the Court about, or about matters connected with, communications or potential communications between the parties that are without prejudice or privileged.

App 4.014   **Exchange of Reports**

> H2.18 In commercial cases the Court will where appropriate direct that the reports of expert witnesses beexchanged sequentially rather than simultaneously. This is an issue that the Court will normally wish to consider at the Case Management Conference.

App 4.015   **Meetings of Expert Witnesses**

> H2.19 A meeting or meetings of expert witnesses before trial will normally be ordered. Sometimes it may be useful for there to be further meetings during the trial itself.

H2.20 The purposes of meetings of experts are to give the experts the opportunity:
a. to discuss the expert issues;
b. to decide, with the benefit of that discussion, on which expert issues they share or can come to agree the same expert opinion and on which expert issues there remains a difference of expert opinion between them (and what that difference is).
(In the Commercial Court this description of the purpose of the meetings takes the place of the description at CPR 35.12(1)).

H2.21 Subject to paragraph H2.24 below, the content of the discussion between the experts at or in connection with x meeting is without prejudice, and in particular (in accprdance with CPR 35.12(4)) shall not be referred to at the trial unless the parties agree.

H2.22 Subject to any directions of the Court, the procedure to be adopted at these meetings is a matter for the experts, not the parties or their legal representatives.

H2.23 Neither the parties nor their legal representatives should seek to restrict the freedom of experts to identify and acknowledge the expert issues on which they agree (i.e. on which they share the same expert opinion) at (or following further consideration after) meetings of experts.

H2.24 At or following their meetings the experts should prepare a joint memorandum for the Court recording:
a. the fact that they have met and discussed the expert issues;
b. the expert issues on which they agree (i.e. on which they share the same expert opinion);
c. the expert issues where they there is a difference of expert opinion between them, and a summary of what that difference of expert opinion is.
(In the Commercial Court this automatic requirement applies notwithstanding the Court's powers under CPR 35.12(3)).

H2.25 Where experts reach agreement on an expert issue during (or following further consideration after) their meetings the agreement shall not bind the parties unless the parties expressly agree to be bound by the agreement.

H2.26 Following the preparation of the joint memorandum each expert may prepare a short supplemental report highlighting the reasons why the expert adheres to the views he does on the expert issues recorded in the memorandum as being issues where there is a difference of expert opinion.

Written Questions to Experts

App 4.016

H2.27 CPR 35.6 contains a procedure allowing a party, without seeking the prior permission of the Court, to put written questions to an expert instructed by another party (or to a single joint expert) about the expert's report. By CPR 35.6(2)(c) the questions must be for the purpose only of clarification of the report unless the Court gives permission or the other party agrees.

H2.28 The Commercial Court will pay close attention to the use of this procedure (especially where separate experts are instructed) to ensure that it remains an instrument for the helpful exchange of information. The Court will not allow it to interfere with the procedure for an exchange of professional opinion at a meeting of experts, or to inhibit that exchange of professional opinion. In cases where (for example) questions that are oppressive in number or content are put, or questions are put (without permission) for any purpose other than clarification of an expert's report, the Court will not hesitate to disallow the questions and to make an appropriate order for costs against the party putting the questions.

App 4.017   Inspection of Documents in an Expert's Report

H2.29   CPR 31.14(e) provides that (subject to CPR 35.10(4)) a party may inspect a document mentioned in an expert's report. In a commercial case an expert's report will frequently, and helpfully, list all or many of the relevant previous papers (published or unpublished) or books written by the expert or to which the expert has contributed. Requiring inspewction of this material may often be unrealistic, and the collating and copying burden could be huge. Accordingly, and subject to paragraph H2.30 below, in the Commercial Court a party wishing to inspect a document in an expert report should (failing agreement) make an application to the Court for that facility. The Court will not accede to the application unless it is satisfied that inspection is appropriate for dealing with the case justly and that the document is not reasonably available to the party making the application from an alternative source.

H2.30   There should however be no need for an application to the Court in the case of photographs, plans, analyses, measurements, survey reports or other similar documents, and any unpublished sources relied on by an expert witness. Unless already provided on inspection of documents at the stage of disclosure, these must be provided to all parties at the same time as the report of the expert.

Trial

H2.31   At trial the evidence of expert witnesses is usually taken as a block, after the evidence of witnesses of fact has been given.

App 4.018   H3 EVIDENCE BY VIDEO LINK

H3.1   In an appropriate case, permission may be given for the oral evidence of a witness to be given by video link. If permission is given the court will give directions for the conduct of this part of the trial.

H3.2   The party seeking permission should prepare and serve on all parties and lodge with the Court a memorandum dealing with the matters outlined in the Videoconferencing Protocol (Appendix 15), and setting out precisely what arrangements are proposed. Where the proposal involves transmission from a location with no existing video link facility, experience shows that the questions of feasibility, timing and cost will require particularly close investigation.

H3.3   The question of permission, and of directions, should be raised at the earliest possible opportunity. It will normally be considered at the Case Management Conference or, at the latest, at any Pre-Trial Review although it is recognised that in some cases it may have to be considered at an even later point.

H3.4   In considering whether to give permission the Court will be concerned in particular to balance any potential savings of costs against the fact that the Court will not, if permission is given, observe the witness at first hand when the witness gives oral testimony.

App 4.019   H4 TAKING EVIDENCE FROM ABROAD

H4.1   In an appropriate case, permission may be given for the evidence of a witness to be taken from abroad. CPR Part 34 contains provisions for the taking of evidence by deposition, and the issue of letters of request.

H4.2   In a very exceptional case, and subject in particular to all necessary approvals being obtained and diplomatic requirements satisfied, the Court may be prepared to consider conducting part of the proceedings abroad where that very exceptional course appears to be necessary. The opportunity for the oral evidence of a witness to be given by video link may well militate against taking this course.

Appendix 5
Extract from the Queen's Bench Guide
7. Case Management and Interim Remedies

7. Case Management and Interim Remedies

7.1 Case management — general:

7.1.1 The CPR require the court to provide a high degree of case management. Case management includes; identifying disputed issues at an early stage; fixing timetables; dealing with as many aspects of the claim as possible on the same occasion; controlling costs; disposing of proceedings summarily where appropriate; dealing with the applications without a hearing where appropriate; and giving directions to ensure that the trial of a claim proceeds quickly and efficiently. The court will expect the parties to co-operate with each other, and where appropriate, will encourage the parties to use ADR or otherwise help them settle the case.

7.1.2 Parties and their legal representatives will be expected to do all that they can to agree proposals for the management of the claim in accordance with Rule 29.4 and paragraphs 4.6 to 4.8 of the Part 29 Practice Direction. There is provision in the Allocation Questionnaire for proposing certain directions to be made, otherwise parties may use form PF 50 for making the application (attaching to it the draft form of order in form PF 52) and file it for the Master's approval. If the Master approves the proposals he will give directions accordingly.

7.1.3 Parties should consider whether a case summary would assist the Master in dealing with the issues before him. Paragraph 5.7 of the Part 29 Practice Direction sets out the provisions for preparation of a case summary.

7.2 The Case Management Conference:

7.2.1 Parties who are unable to agree proposals for the management of the case, should notify the Court of the matters which they are unable to agree.

7.2.2 Where;

    (1) the parties proposed directions are not approved, or

(2) parties are unable to agree proposed directions, or

(3) the Master wishes to make further directions,

the Master will generally either consult the parties or direct that a case management conference be held.

7.2.3 In relatively straightforward claims, the Court will give directions without holding a case management conference.

7.2.4 Any party who considers that a case management conference should be held before any directions are given should so state in his Allocation Questionnaire, (or in a Part 8 claim should notify the Master in writing), giving his reasons and supplying a realistic time estimate for the case management conference, with a list of any dates or times convenient to all parties, or most of them, in form PF 49.

7.2.5 Where a case management conference has been fixed, parties should ensure that any other applications are listed or made at that hearing. A party applying for directions at the case management conference should use form PF 50 for making their application and attach to it the draft order for directions (form PF 52).

7.2.6 The advocates instructed or expected to be instructed to appear at the trial should attend any hearing at which case management directions are likely to be given. In any event, the legal representatives who attend the case management conference must be familiar with the case and have sufficient authority to deal with any issues which may arise. Where necessary, the court may order the attendance of a party.

7.3 Preliminary issues:

App 5.004   7.3.1 Costs can sometimes be saved by identifying decisive issues, or potentially decisive issues, and by the Court ordering that they be tried first. The decision of one issue, although not necessarily itself decisive of the claim as a whole, may enable the parties to settle the remainder of the dispute. In such a case, the trial of a preliminary issue may be appropriate.

7.3.2 At the allocation stage, at any case management conference and again at any pre-trial review, the court will consider whether the trial of a preliminary issue may be helpful. Where such an order is made, the parties and the court should consider whether the costs of the issue should be in the issue or in the claim as a whole.

7.3.3 Where there is an application for summary judgment, and issues of law or construction may be determined in the respondent's favour, it will usually be in the interests of the parties for such issues to be determined conclusively, rather than that the application should simply be dismissed.

7.4 Trial timetable:

App 5.005   7.4.1 To assist the court to set a trial timetable, a draft timetable should be prepared by the claimant's advocate(s) after consulting the other parties advocates. If there are differing views, those differences should be clearly indicated in the timetable. The draft timetable should be filed with the trial bundle.

7.4.2 The trial timetable will normally include times for giving evidence (whether of fact or opinion) and for oral submissions during the trial.

7.4.3 The trial timetable may be fixed at the case management conference, at any pre-trial review or at the beginning of the trial itself.

7.5 Listing Questionnaire:

App 5.006   7.5.1 The court may send out a Listing Questionnaire (N170) to all parties for completion, specifying the date by which it must be returned. The Master will then fix the trial date or period ("the trial window"). It is likely however, that the Master will already have sufficient information to enable him to fix a trial window, and will dispense with the need for a Listing Questionnaire subject to any requirement of the Clerk of the Lists for one to be filed. Instead, the Master will direct the parties within a specified time to attend before the Clerk of the Lists to fix a trial date within that window.

7.5.2 Paragraph 6.4 of the Costs Practice Direction requires an estimate of costs to be filed and served with the Listing Questionnaire. If the filing of a Listing Questionnaire has been dispensed with, the estimate of costs should be filed on attendance before the Clerk of the Lists.

7.6 Pre-trial review:

7.6.1 Where the trial of a claim is estimated to last more than 10 days, or where the circumstances require it, the Master may direct that a pre-trial review ("PTR") should be held. The PTR may be heard by a Master, but more usually is heard by a Judge.

App 5.007

7.6.2 Application should normally be made to the Clerk of the Lists for the PTR to be heard by the trial judge (if known), and the applicant should do all that he can to ensure that it is heard between 8 and 4 weeks before the trial date, and in any event long enough before the trial date to allow a realistic time in which to complete any outstanding matters.

7.6.3 The PTR should be attended by the advocates who are to represent the parties at the trial.

7.6.4 At least 7 days before the date fixed for the PTR, the applicant must serve the other parties with a list of matters to be considered at the PTR, and those other parties must serve their responses at least 2 days before the PTR. Account must be taken of the answers in any listing questionnaires filed. Realistic proposals must be put forward and if possible agreed as to the time likely to be required for each stage of the trial and as to the order in which witnesses are to be called.

7.6.5 The applicant should lodge a properly indexed bundle containing the listing questionnaires (if directed to be filed) and the lists of matters and the proposals, together with the results of discussions between the parties, and any other relevant material, in the Listing Office, Room WG5, by no later than 10.00am on the day before the day fixed for the hearing of the PTR. If the PTR is to take place before a Master and he asks for the bundle in advance, it should be lodged in the Masters' Support Unit, Room E14. Otherwise it should be lodged at the hearing.

7.6.6 At the PTR, the court will review the parties' state of preparation, deal with any outstanding matters, and give any directions or further directions that may be necessary.

7.7 Requests for further information:

7.7.1 A party seeking further information or clarification under Part 18 should serve a written request on the party from whom the information is sought before making an application to the court. Paragraph 1 of the Part 18 Practice Direction deals with how the request should be made, and paragraph 2 deals with the response. A response should be verified by a statement of truth. Parties may use form PF 56 for a combined request and reply, if they so wish.

App 5.008

7.7.2 If a party who has been asked to provide further information or clarification objects or is unable to do so, he must notify the party making the request in writing.

7.7.3 Where it is necessary to apply for an order for further information or clarification the party making the application should set out in or have attached to his application notice;

(1) the text of the order sought specifying the matters on which further information or clarification is sought, and

(2) whether a request has been made and, if so, the result of that request.

Applicants may use form PF 57 for their application notice.

7.8 Disclosure:

App 5.009   7.8.1 Under Part 31, there is no longer any general duty to disclose documents. Instead, a party is prevented from relying on any document that he has not disclosed, and is required to give inspection of any document to which he refers in his statement of case or in any witness statement, etc.. The intention is that disclosure should be proportionate to the value of the claim.

7.8.2 If an order for disclosure is made, unless the contrary is stated, the Court will order standard disclosure, namely disclosure of only;

(1) the documents on which a party relies,

(2) the documents that adversely affect his own or another party's case,

(3) the documents that support another party's case, and

(4) the documents required to be disclosed by a relevant practice direction.

Parties should give standard disclosure by completing form N265 but may also list documents by category.

7.8.3 The court may either limit or dispense with disclosure (and the parties may agree to do likewise). The court may also order disclosure of specified documents or specified classes of documents. In deciding whether to make any such order for specific disclosure, the court will want to be satisfied that the disclosure is necessary, that the cost of disclosure will not outweigh the benefits of disclosure and that a party's ability to continue the litigation would not be impaired by any such order.

7.8.4 The court will therefore seek to ensure that any specific disclosure ordered is appropriate to the particular case, taking into account the financial position of the parties, the importance of the case and the complexity of the issues.

7.8.5 If specific disclosure is sought, a separate application for specific disclosure should be made in accordance with Part 23; it is not a matter that would be routinely dealt with at the CMC. The parties should give careful thought to ways of limiting the burdens of such disclosure, whether by giving disclosure in stages, by dispensing with the need to produce copies of the same document, by requiring disclosure of documents sufficient merely for a limited purpose, or otherwise. They should also consider whether the need for disclosure could be reduced or eliminated by a request for further information.

7.8.6 A party who has the right to inspect a document should give written notice of his wish to inspect to the party disclosing the document. That party must permit inspection not more than 7 days after receipt of the notice.

7.9 Experts and Assessors:

App 5.010   7.9.1 The parties in a claim must bear in mind that under Part 35 no party may call an expert or put in evidence an expert's report without the court's express permission, and the court is under a duty to restrict such evidence to what is reasonably required.

7.9.2 The duty of an expert called to give evidence is to assist the court. This duty overrides any obligation to the party instructing him or by whom he is being paid (see the Part 35 Practice Direction). In fulfilment of this duty, an expert must for instance make it clear if a particular question or issue falls outside his expertise or if he considers that insufficient information is available on which to express an opinion.

7.9.3 Before the Master gives permission, he must be told the field of expertise of the expert on whose evidence a party wishes to rely and where practicable the identity of the expert. Even then, he may, before giving permission, impose a limit on the extent to which the cost of such evidence may be recovered from the other parties in the claim.

7.9.4 Parties should always consider whether a single expert could be appointed in a particular claim or to deal with a particular issue. Before giving permission for the parties to call separate experts, the Master will always consider whether a single joint expert ought to be used, whether in relation to the issues as a whole or to a particular issue.

7.9.5 In very many cases it is possible for the question of expert evidence to be dealt with by a single expert. Single experts are, for example, often appropriate to deal with questions of quantum in cases where primary issues are as to liability. Likewise, where expert evidence is required in order to acquaint the court with matters of expert fact, as opposed to opinion, a single expert will usually be appropriate. There remain, however, a body of cases where liability will turn upon expert opinion evidence and where it will be appropriate for the parties to instruct their own experts. For example, in cases where the issue for determination is as to whether a party acted in accordance with proper professional standards, it will often be of value to the court to hear the opinions of more than one expert as to the proper standard in order that the court becomes acquainted with a range of views existing upon the question and in order that the evidence can be tested in cross-examination.

7.9.6 It will not be a sufficient ground for objecting to an order for a single joint expert that the parties have already chosen their own experts. An order for a single joint expert does not prevent a party from having his own expert to advise him, though that is likely to be at his own cost, regardless of the outcome.

7.9.7 When the use of a single joint expert is being considered, the Master will expect the parties to co-operate in agreeing terms of reference for the expert. In most cases, such terms of reference will include a statement of what the expert is asked to do, will identify any documents that he will be asked to consider and will specify any assumptions that he is asked to make.

7.9.8 The court will generally also order that experts in the same field confer on a 'without prejudice' basis, and then report in writing to the parties and the court on the extent of any agreement, giving reasons at least in summary for any continuing disagreement. A direction to 'confer' gives the experts the choice of discussing the matter by telephone or in any other convenient way, as an alternative to attending an actual meeting. Any material change of view of an expert should be communicated in writing to the other parties through their legal representatives, and when appropriate, to the court.

7.9.9 Written questions may be put to an expert within 28 days after service of his report, but are for purposes of clarification of the expert's report when the other party does not understand it. Questions going beyond this can only be put with the agreement of the parties or the Master's permission. The procedure of putting written questions to experts is not intended to interfere with the procedure for an exchange of professional opinion in discussions between experts or to inhibit that exchange of professional opinion. If questions that are oppressive in number or content are put without permission for any purpose other than clarification of the expert's report, the court is likely to disallow the questions and make an appropriate order for costs against the party putting them. (See paragraph 4.3 of the Part 35 Practice Direction with respect to payment of an expert's fees for answering questions under Rule 35.6.)

7.9.10 An expert may file with the court a written request for directions to assist him in carrying out his function as an expert. The expert should guard against accidentally informing the court about, or about matters connected with, communications or potential communications between the parties that are without prejudice or privileged. The expert may properly be asked to be privy to the content of these communications because he has been asked to assist the party instructing him to evaluate them.

7.9.11 Under Rule 35.15 the court may appoint an assessor to assist it in relation to any matter in which the assessor has skill and experience. The report of the assessor is made available to the parties. The remuneration of the assessor is decided by the court and forms part of the costs of the proceedings.

7.10 Evidence:

7.10.1 Evidence is dealt with in the CPR in Parts 32, 33 and 34.   **App 5.011**

7.10.2 The most common form of written evidence is a witness statement. The Part 32 Practice Direction at paragraphs 17, 18 and 19 contains information about the heading, body (what it must contain) and format of a witness statement. The witness must sign a statement of truth to verify the witness statement; the wording of the statement of truth is set out in paragraph 20.2 of the Practice Direction.

7.10.3 A witness statement may be used as evidence in support of an interim application and, where it has been served on any other party to a claim, it may be relied on as a statement of the oral evidence of the witness at the trial. Part 33 contains provisions relating to the use of hearsay evidence in a witness statement.

7.10.4 In addition to the information and provisions for making a witness statement mentioned in paragraph 7.10.2, the following matters should be borne in mind;

(1) a witness statement must contain the truth, the whole truth and nothing but the truth on the issues it covers,

(2) those issues should consist only of the issues on which the party serving the witness statement wishes that witness to give evidence in chief and should not include commentary on the trial bundle or other matters which may arise during the trial,

(3) a witness statement should be as concise as the circumstances allow, inadmissible or irrelevant material should not be included,

(4) the cost of preparation of an over-elaborate witness statement may not be allowed,

(5) Rule 32.14 states that proceedings for contempt of court may be brought against a person if he makes, or causes to be made, a false statement in a document verified by a statement of truth without an honest belief in its truth,

(6) if a party discovers that a witness statement which they have served is incorrect they must inform the other parties immediately.

7.10.5 Evidence may also be given by affidavit but unless an affidavit is specifically required either in compliance with a court order, a Rule or Practice Direction, or an enactment, the party putting forward the affidavit may not recover from another party the cost of making an affidavit unless the court so orders.

7.10.6 The Part 32 Practice Direction at paragraphs 3 to 6 contains information about the heading, body, jurat (the sworn statement which authenticates the affidavit) and the format of an affidavit. The court will normally give directions as to whether a witness statement or, where appropriate, an affidavit is to be filed.

7.10.7 A statement of case which has been verified by a statement of truth and an application notice containing facts which have been verified by a statement of truth may also stand as evidence other than at the trial.

7.10.8 Evidence by deposition is dealt with in Part 34. A party may apply to a Master for an order for a person to be examined before a hearing takes place (Rule 34.8). Evidence obtained on an examination under that Rule is referred to as a deposition. The Master may order the person to be examined before either a Judge, an examiner of the court or such other person as the court appoints. The Part 34 Practice Direction at paragraph 4 sets out in detail how the examination should take place.

7.10.9 Provisions relating to applications for evidence by deposition to be taken either;

(1) in this country for use in a foreign court, or

(2) abroad for use in proceedings within the jurisdiction

are set out in detail in the Part 34 Practice Direction at paragraphs 5 and 6.

7.10.10 The procedure for issuing a witness summons is also dealt with in Part 34 and the Practice Direction. A witness summons may require a witness to;

(1) attend court,

(2) produce documents to the court, or

(3) both,

on either a date fixed for the hearing or another date as the court may direct (but see also Rule 31.17 which may be used when there are areas of contention).

7.10.11 The court may also issue a witness summons in aid of a court or tribunal which does not have the power to issue a witness summons in relation to the proceedings before it (and see the Part 34 Practice Direction at paragraphs 1, 2 and 3).

7.10.12 To issue a witness summons, two copies should be filed in the Action Department, Room E14 for sealing; one copy will be retained on the court file.

7.11 Hearings:

Hearings generally

7.11.1 All hearings are in principle open to the public, even though in practice most of the hearings until the trial itself will be attended only by the parties and their representatives. However, in an appropriate case the court may decide to hold a hearing in private. Rule 39.2 lists the circumstances where it may be appropriate to hold a hearing in private. In addition, paragraph 1.5 of the Part 39 Practice Direction sets out certain types of hearings which may be listed in private.   **App 5.012**

7.11.2 The court also has the power under section 11 of the Contempt of Court Act 1981 to make an order forbidding publication of any details that might identify one or more of the parties. Such orders are granted only in exceptional cases.

7.11.3 References in the CPR and Practice Directions to hearings being in public or private do not restrict any existing rights of audience or confer any new rights of audience in respect of applications or proceedings which under the rules previously in force would have been heard in court or chambers respectively.Advocates (and judges) do not wear robes at interim hearings before High Court Judges, including appeals from Masters, District Judges and the county courts. Robes are worn for trials and certain other proceedings such as preliminary issues, committals etc. It is not intended that the new routes of appeal should restrict the advocate's right of audience, in tha, a solicitor who appeared in a county court matter which is the subject of an appeal to a High Court Judge would normally be allowed to appear at the appeal hearing.

7.11.4 Parties are reminded that they are expected to act with courtesy and respect for the other parties present and for the proceedings of the court. Punctuality is particularly important; being late for hearings is unfair to the other parties and other court users, as well as being discourteous to them and to the court.

Preparation for hearings

7.11.5 To ensure court time is used efficiently there must be adequate preparation prior to the hearing. This includes the preparation and exchange of skeleton arguments, the compilation of bundles of documents and giving realistic time estimates. Where estimates prove inaccurate, a hearing may have to be adjourned to a later date, and the party responsible for the adjournment is likely to be ordered to pay the costs thrown away.   **App 5.013**

7.11.6 The parties should use their best endeavours to agree beforehand the issues, or main issues between them, and must co-operate with the court and each other to enable the court to deal with claims justly; parties may expect to be penalised for failing to do so.

7.11.7 A bundle of documents must be compiled for the court's use at the trial, and also for hearings before the Interim Applications Judge or a Master where the documents to be referred to total 25 pages or more. The party lodging a trial bundle should supply identical bundles to all parties and for the use of witnesses. The efficient preparation of bundles is very important. Where bundles have been properly prepared, the claim will be easier to understand and present, and time and costs are likely to be saved. Where documents are copied unnecessarily or bundled incompetently, the costs may be disallowed. Paragraph 3 of the Part 39 Practice Direction sets out in full the requirements for compiling bundles of documents for hearings or trial.

7.11.8 The trial bundle must be filed not more than 7 and not less than 3 days before the start of the trial. Bundles for a Master's hearing should be brought to the hearing unless the Master directs otherwise. The contents of the trial bundle should be agreed where possible, and it should be made clear whether in addition, they are agreeing that the documents in the bundle are authentic even if not previously disclosed and are evidence of the facts stated in them even if a notice under the Civil Evidence Act 1995 has not been served.

7.11.9 Lists of authorities for use at trial or at substantial hearings before a Judge should be provided to the usher by 9.00am on the first day of the hearing. For other applications before a Judge, or applications before a Master, copies of the authorities should be included in the bundle.

7.11.10 For trial and most hearings before a Judge, and substantial hearings before a Master, a chronology, a list of the persons involved and a list of the issues should be prepared and filed with the skeleton argument. A chronology should be non-contentious and agreed with the other parties if possible. If there is a material dispute about any event stated in the chronology, that should be stated.

7.11.11 Skeleton arguments should be prepared and filed;

(1) for trials, not less than 2 days before the trial in the Listing Office, and

(2) for substantial applications or appeals, not later than 1 day before the hearing in the Listing Office and, where the Master has requested papers in advance of the hearing, in the Masters' Support Unit Room E16.

7.11.12 A skeleton argument should;

(1) concisely summarise the party's submissions in relation to each of the issues,

(2) cite the main authorities relied on, which may be attached,

(3) contain a reading list and an estimate of the time it will take the Judge to read,

(4) be as brief as the issues allow and not normally be longer than 20 pages of double-spaced A4 paper,

(5) be divided into numbered paragraphs and paged consecutively,

(6) avoid formality and use understandable abbreviations, and

(7) identify any core documents which it would be helpful to read beforehand.

7.11.13 Where a party decides not to call a witness whose witness statement has been served, to give oral evidence at trial, prompt notice of this decision should be given to all other parties. The party should also indicate whether he proposes to put, or seek to put, the witness statement in as hearsay evidence. If he does not, any other party may do so.

Recording of proceedings

App 5.014   7.11.14 At any hearing, including the trial, any oral evidence, the judgment or decision (including reasons) and any summing up to a jury will be recorded. At hearings before Masters, it is not normally practicable to record anything other than oral evidence and any judgment, but these will be recorded. A party to the proceedings may obtain a transcript of the proceedings on payment of the appropriate charge, from the Mechanical Recording Department, Room WG5. A person who is not a party to the proceedings may not obtain a transcript of a hearing which took place in private without the permission of the court.

7.11.15 No person or party may use unofficial recording equipment at a hearing without the permission of the court; to do so constitutes a contempt of court.

7.12 Applications:

App 5.015   7.12.1 Applications for court orders are governed by Part 23 and the Part 23 Practice Direction. Rule 23.6 and paragraph 2 of the Part 23 Practice Direction set out the matters an application notice must include. The Part 23 Practice Direction states that form N244 may be used, however, parties may prefer to use form PF244 which is available for use in the Royal Courts of Justice only. To make an application the applicant must file an application notice unless a Rule or Practice Direction permits otherwise or the court dispenses with the requirement for an application notice. Except in cases of extreme urgency, or where giving notice might frustrate the order (as with a search order), an application notice must be served on every party unless a Rule or Practice Direction or a court order dispenses with service (see paragraph 7.12.3 below).

7.12.2 Applications for remedies which a Master has jurisdiction to grant should ordinarily be made to a Master. The Part 2 Practice Direction (Allocation of cases to levels of Judiciary) contains information about the types of applications which may be dealt with by Masters and Judges. An application notice for hearing by;

(1) a Judge should be issued in the Listing Office, Room WG5, and

(2) a Master should be issued in the Masters' Support Unit, Room E16,

and wherever possible should be accompanied by a draft in double spacing of the order sought.

7.12.3 The following are examples of applications which may be heard by a Master where service of the application notice is not required;

(1) service by an alternative method (Rule 6.8),

(2) service of a Claim Form out of the jurisdiction (section III of Part 6),

(3) default judgment under Rule 12.11(4) or (5),

(4) substituting a party under Rule 19.1(4),

(5) permission to issue a witness summons under Rule 34.3(2),

(6) deposition for use in a foreign court (Schedule 1 to the CPR - RSC O.70),

(7) charging order to show cause (Schedule 1 to the CPR - RSC O.50 r.1(2)), and

(8) garnishee order to show cause (Schedule 1 to the CPR - RSC O.49 r.2(1).

7.12.4 Paragraph 3 of the Part 23 Practice Direction states in addition that an application may be made without serving an application notice;

(1) where there is exceptional urgency,

(2) where the overriding objective is best furthered by doing so,

(3) by consent of all parties, and

(4) where a date for a hearing has been fixed and a party wishes to make an application at that hearing but does not have sufficient time to serve an application notice.

With the court's permission an application may also be made without serving an application notice where secrecy is essential.

7.12.5 Where an application is heard in the absence of one or more of the parties, it is the duty of the party attending to disclose fully all matters relevant to the application, even those matters adverse to the applicant. Failure to do so may result in the order being set aside. Any party who does not attend a hearing may apply to have the order set aside.

7.12.6 Where notice of an application is to be given, the application notice should be served as soon as practicable after issue and, if there is to be a hearing, at least 3 clear days before the hearing date. Where there is insufficient time to serve an application notice, informal notice of the application should be given unless the circumstances of the application require secrecy.

7.12.7 The court may deal with an application without a hearing if;

(1) the parties agree the terms of the order sought,

(2) the parties agree that the application should be dealt with without a hearing, or

(3) the court does not consider that a hearing would be appropriate.

7.12.8 The court may deal with an application or part of an application by telephone where it is convenient to do so or in matters of extreme urgency. See paragraph 6 of the Part 23 Practice Direction and paragraph 4.5 of the Part 25 Practice Direction (Interim Injunctions).

7.12.9 Applications of extreme urgency may be made out of hours and will be dealt with by the duty judge. An explanation will be required as to why it was not made or could not be made during normal court hours.

7.12.10 Initial contact should be made through the Security Office on 020 7947 6260 who will require the applicants phone number. The clerk to the duty judge will then contact the applicant and will require the following information;

(1) the name of the party on whose behalf the application is to be made,

(2) the name and status of the person making the application,

(3) the nature of the application,

(4) the degree of urgency, and

(5) the contact telephone number(s).

7.12.11 The duty judge will indicate to his clerk if he thinks it appropriate for the application to be dealt with by telephone or in court. The clerk will inform the applicant and make the necessary arrangements. Where the duty judge decides to deal with the application by telephone, and the facility is available, it is likely that the judge will require a draft order to be faxed to him. An application for an injunction will be dealt with by telephone only where the applicant is represented by counsel or solicitors.

7.12.12 It is not normally possible to seal an order out of hours. The judge is likely to order the applicant to file the application notice and evidence in support on the same or next working day, together with two copies of the order for sealing.

7.13 Interim remedies:

App 5.016

7.13.1 Interim remedies which the court may grant are listed in Rule 25.1. An order for an interim remedy may be made at any time including before proceedings are started and after judgment has been given. Some of the most commonly sought remedies are injunctions, most of which are heard by the Interim Applications Judge.

7.13.2 An application notice for an injunction should be filed in the Listing Office, Room WG5, and may be made without giving notice to the other parties in the first instance. This is most likely to be appropriate in applications for search orders and freezing injunctions which may also be heard in private if the judge thinks it appropriate to do so. Where the injunction is granted without the other party being present it will normally be for a limited period, seldom more than 7 days. The Part 25 (Interim Injunctions) Practice Direction at paragraph 4 deals fully with making urgent applications and those without notice, and paragraphs 6, 7 and 8 deal specifically with search orders and freezing injunctions, examples of which are annexed to the Practice Direction.

7.13.3 Applications for interim payments are heard by a Master. The application notice should be filed in the Masters' Support Unit, Room E14. The requirements for obtaining an order for an interim payment are fully dealt with in the Part 25 (Interim Payments) Practice Direction.

Appendix 6
Extract from the Chancery Division Guide
Chapter 4 Disclosure of Documents and Expert Evidence

Key Rules: CPR Part 18, 29, 31 and 35; PDs supplementing CPR Part 31 and 35

4.1 As part of its management of a case, the court will give directions about the disclosure of documents and any expert evidence. Attention is drawn to paragraphs 3.7 to 3.9 above. An application for specific disclosure should be made by a specific Part 23 application and is not to be regarded as a matter routinely dealt with at a case management conference. **App 6.001**

Disclosure of Documents

General

4.2 Under the CPR, the normal order for disclosure is an order for standard disclosure, that is, disclosure of: **App 6.002**

(1) a party's own documents — that is, the documents on which a party relies;

(2) adverse documents — that is, documents which adversely affect his or her own or another party's case or support another party's case; and

(3) required documents — that is, documents which a practice direction requires him or her to disclose.

4.3 The court may make an order for specific disclosure going beyond the limits of standard disclosure if it is satisfied that standard disclosure is inadequate.

4.4 The court will not make such an order readily. One of the clear principles underlying the CPR is that the burden and cost of disclosure should be reduced. The court will, therefore seek to ensure that any specific disclosure ordered is proportionate in the sense that the cost of such disclosure does not outweigh the benefits to be obtained from such disclosure. The court will, accordingly, seek to tailor the order for disclosure to the requirements of the particular case. The financial position of the parties, the importance of the case and the complexity of the issues will be taken into account when considering whether more than standard disclosure should be ordered.

4.5 If specific disclosure is sought, the parties should give careful thought to the ways in which such disclosure can be limited, for example by requiring disclosure in stages or by requiring disclosure simply of sufficient documents to show a specified matter and so on. They should also consider whether the need for disclosure could be avoided by requiring a party to provide information under Part 18.

Expert Evidence

General

4.6 Part 35 contains particular provisions designed to limit the amount of expert evidence to be placed before the court and to reinforce the obligation of impartiality which is imposed upon an expert witness. **App 6.003**

4.7 Fundamentally, Part 35 states that expert evidence must be restricted to what is reasonably required to resolve the proceedings and makes provision for the court to direct that expert evidence is given by a single joint expert. The key question now in relation to expert evidence is the question as to what added value such evidence will provide to the court in its determination of a given case.

Duties of an expert

App 6.004

4.8 It is the duty of an expert to help the court on the matters within his or her expertise; this duty overrides any obligation to the person from whom the expert has received instructions or by whom he or she is paid (rule 35.3). Attention is drawn to the PD — Experts and Assessors supplementing Part 35.

4.9 In fulfilment of this duty, an expert must for instance make it clear if a particular question or issue falls outside his or her expertise or he or she considers that insufficient data is available on which to express an opinion. Any material change of view by an expert should be communicated in writing (through legal representatives) to the other parties without delay, and when appropriate to the court.

Single joint expert

App 6.005

4.10 The introduction to the PD — Experts and Assessors supplementing Part 35 states that, where possible, matters requiring expert evidence should be dealt with by a single expert.

4.11 In very many cases it is possible for the question of expert evidence to be dealt with by a single expert. Single experts are, for example, often appropriate to deal with questions of quantum in cases where the primary issues are as to liability. Likewise, where expert evidence is required in order to acquaint the court with matters of expert fact, as opposed to opinion, a single expert will usually be appropriate. There remains, however, a body of cases where liability will turn upon expert opinion evidence and where it will be appropriate for the parties to instruct their own experts. For example, in cases where the issue for determination is as to whether a party acted in accordance with proper professional standards, it will often be of value to the court to hear the opinions of more than one expert as to the proper standard in order that the court becomes acquainted with the range of views existing upon the question and in order that the evidence can be tested in cross examination.

4.12 It is not necessarily a sufficient objection to the making by the court of an order for a single joint expert that the parties have already appointed their own experts. An order for a single joint expert does not prevent a party from having his or her own expert to advise him or her, but he or she may well be unable to recover the cost of employing his or her own expert from the other party. The duty of an expert who is called to give evidence is to help the court.

4.13 When the use of a single joint expert is contemplated the court will expect the parties to co-operate in developing and agreeing to the greatest possible extent, terms of reference for the expert. In most cases the terms of reference will (in particular) detail what the expert is asked to do, identify any documentary material he or she is asked to consider and specify any assumptions he or she is asked to make.

More than one expert — exchange of reports

App 6.006

4.14 In an appropriate case the court will direct that experts' reports are delivered sequentially.

Discussion between experts

App 6.007

4.15 The court will normally direct discussion between experts before trial. Sometimes it may be useful for there to be further discussions during the trial itself. The purpose of these discussions is to give the experts the opportunity:

(1) to discuss the expert issues; and

(2) to identify the expert issues on which they share the same opinion and those on which there remains a difference of opinion between them (and what that difference is).

4.16 Unless the court otherwise directs, the procedure to be adopted at these discussions is a matter for the experts. It may be sufficient if the discussion takes place by telephone.

4.17 Parties must not seek to restrict their expert's participation in any discussion directed by the court, but they are not bound by any agreement on any issue reached by their expert unless they expressly so agree.

Written questions to experts

4.18 It is emphasised that this procedure is only for the purpose (generally) of seeking clarification of an expert's report where the other party is unable to understand it. Written questions going beyond this can only be put with the agreement of the parties or with the permission of the court. The procedure of putting written questions to experts is not intended to interfere with the procedure for an exchange of professional opinion in discussions between experts or to inhibit that exchange of professional opinion. If questions that are oppressive in number or content are put or questions are put without permission for any purpose other than clarification of an expert's report, the court will not hesitate to disallow the questions and to make an appropriate order for costs against the party putting them.

App 6.008

Request by an expert to the court for directions

4.19 An expert may file with the court a written request for directions to assist him or her in carrying out his or her function as expert: rule 35.14. The expert should guard against accidentally informing the court about, or about matters connected with, communications or potential communications between the parties that are without prejudice or privileged. The expert may properly be privy to the content of these communications because he or she has been asked to assist the party instructing him or her to evaluate them.

App 6.009

Assessors

4.20 Under rule 35.15 the court may appoint an assessor to assist it in relation to any matter in which the assessor has skill and experience. The report of the assessor is made available to the parties. The remuneration of the assessor is determined by the court and forms part of the costs of the proceedings.

App 6.010